TEAMING
FOR
IMPROVEMENT

TEAMING
FOR
IMPROVEMENT

Getting Results in the Millennium

William Stieber, Ph.D.

BookPartners
Wilsonville, Oregon

Cartoons included in this book are reprinted with permission. DILBERT © reprinted by permission of United Feature Syndicate.

"Any Road Will Do" © reprinted by permission of Tool Thyme for Trainers.

Library of Congress Cataloging-in-Publication Data

Stieber, William, 1950–
    Teaming for improvement : getting results in the millenium / William Stieber
        p.   cm.
    Includes bibliographical references (p.).
    ISBN 1-885221-85-1 (trade pbk.)
    1. Teams in the workplace. 2. Total quality management.
I. Title.
HD66.S75   1999
658.4'036--dc21   99-34264
                                                                        CIP

Cover design by Richard Ferguson
Text design by Sheryl Mehary

BookPartners, Inc.
P. O. Box 922
Wilsonville, Oregon 97071

*To my wife Loretta
and my sons Michael and Jeffrey,
for their continued love and support.*

CONTENTS

ACKNOWLEDGMENTS

This book began as a personal goal during the early phase of establishing my own business. It moved from goal to reality only at the urging of some very special people and by virtue of experiences I gained with various clients.

A very deep and heartfelt thank you goes out to my good friends and ongoing clients, particularly those at SmithKline Beecham. Many SmithKline Beecham members not only allowed me to reflect on some positive teaming experiences but also participated in a number of interviews I conducted along the journey. My thanks to my friend Marilyn Odesser-Torpey, who read early drafts of the manuscript and gave me feedback; to Ginger Marlowe at BookPartners, for her guidance and support in producing the book; and to my many professional colleagues at the Liberty Bell Speakers Association, National Speakers Association, and the Association for Quality and Participation, who helped not only with suggestions but also with continual inquiry about the book's progress, which served as a catalyst in completing its content.

Special thank yous go to the many organizations, too numerous to mention, that allowed me to participate in the small- and large-scale improvement efforts that provided me with many of the examples used in this book. My apologies to all of the other people who have helped, and whose names have not been mentioned; you are not forgotten.

PREFACE

How did:

- A global pharmaceutical giant improve processes enough to save millions of dollars, increase creativity and generally sharpen its competitive edge in the global marketplace?
- A middle-sized manufacturer of vending machines achieve a 20 percent improvement in quality?
- A financial subsidiary of a major telecommunications firm produce a 33 percent increase in customer satisfaction, a fivefold increase in profits over the last five years, and a working environment for employees that is regarded as one of the best in the industry?
- The U.S. hockey team win a major victory over the Russian team at the 1980 Olympics?

As a consultant and facilitator for companies all over the world, I was involved in helping three out of these four organizations find the key to success in today's competitive world—and prepare for success in the increasingly competitive world of the future. (I'd like to say that I also had a hand in the U.S. Olympic hockey victory, but the team was well able to accomplish that feat without my help.) All four of these organizations have found the secret that everyone is looking for. They have discovered the power of teams.

I'm not talking about a lip service pledge of allegiance to teamwork. I am referring to a real commitment to teams—from their creation, through their development, to the accomplishment of well-planned, company-supported goals.

Now, I don't blame you if the use of a corporate buzzword makes you cringe. We all know that buzzwords are usually nothing more than euphemisms used to sugarcoat something unpleasant. You find buzzwords in all professions and all parts of life. In war, casualties are often reported as "collateral damage" to minimize the natural emotional reaction to the loss of human lives. In medicine, an operation seems a lot less dramatic when it's called a "procedure." However, when buzzwords become part of the common everyday vernacular, they can lose their soothing effect. In fact, some can eventually take on negative meanings of their own.

Take the buzzwords "reengineering" and "restructuring." Both words were created to take some of the sting out of change. Although they may have originated with two distinct definitions, over time they have become interchangeable. And why not? For many people, both have had the same bottom line meaning— "You're fired!"

Teams, teaming, teamwork. These sound good. And they are good. You could call the teaming process "putting our heads together to find solutions" or "pooling ideas and creativity to achieve success for all." It isn't important what you call it as long as you do it. For yourself, think of teaming as the key to more positive involvement, more empowerment and more self-management. For your company, think of it as the key to the constant improvement necessary for leadership in the coming years.

The word "team" can refer to a variety of different structures with a variety of different purposes. There are design or reengineering teams (here that infamous buzzword takes on a purely positive meaning). These teams are involved in the design and implementation of radical structural, organizational and systems improvement. Then there are quality or process improvement teams that help organizations incrementally improve by designing and redesigning processes and eliminating wastes. These teams are also referred to as CATs, PITs, Continuous Improvement Teams, Quality Action Teams, Continuous Action Teams, Quality Improvement Teams, and other creative designations. It doesn't matter what you call it. A quality or process improvement team by any other name can get the job done just as efficiently and effectively.

Another type of ad hoc team is the project team. The goal of the project team is very specific. For example, a project team may be created solely for the purpose of launching a new product. Project teams may be cross-functional, bringing together people who perform various functions throughout the company. Some companies also use virtual project teams that use technology to communicate.

Finally, there are self-directed or self-managed teams, the utopia of teams because they are able to play a major role in the running of their organizations without becoming ensnared in the traditional multilayered management structures (a handy euphemism for "bureaucracies"). Some self-directed teams become permanent fixtures involved in the daily running of the business. Others, such as ad hoc design and quality improvement teams, are actually created to have a finite lifespan. These types of temporary teams are often instrumental in developing the designs and implementing the changes that lead to either incremental or radical improvement in a wide range of business processes and procedures. In companies in which these improvement teams have been supported in their development and work, results have included increased customer, community and employee satisfaction, and increased revenues due to increased sales and/or significant decreases in the cost of doing business.

All very positive stuff, right? Well, before you go charging into work tomorrow to share your revelation that teams are the answer to "What's the meaning of life?" (or the meaning of business in the new millennium), let me offer an important caveat. Just because you get a group of people together and call that group a team, it doesn't mean that improvement is guaranteed. Look at it this way: If you get twenty-two big guys together and throw them a football, do you think you'll automatically have a Super Bowl-winning team? Or that Olympic Gold Medal-winning hockey team—do you think all they needed was skates and helmets to make them such formidable competitors?

Team spirit is a wondrous thing, but it can only take you so far. A group of football or hockey players can only become a real team when they know the same game rules, learn the same plays, understand the strengths and weaknesses of their teammates...you get the idea.

The same goes for work teams. Whether a particular team's purpose is to achieve continuous improvement or more radical improvement within an organization, the members and company management need to employ some basic elements and techniques of team building and development before they can hope to make any positive impact on the business.

During my career, I have heard some pretty terrible horror stories about half-baked attempts to introduce teams into some organizations. Someone in each organization obviously heard or read somewhere that teaming was a good idea. Not understanding that teaming takes a strong company-wide commitment, a great deal of planning and a clear vision of the future, these "innovators" simply collected people into groups, dubbed the groups "teams" and set them to work. What were they to work on? That wasn't important. Part of their job was to figure out what they were supposed to be doing. Sounds a little silly, doesn't it? But, in many instances, that's exactly the way the concept of teams was introduced into organizations.

It isn't hard to understand why, more often than not, this method of launching teams led not to improvement, but to unenthusiastic or confused attempts at compliance at best to absolute disaster at worst. As a result, many companies hastily abandoned their foundering teams and retreated in defeat to their original bureaucratic structures. Your teams do not have to meet this same sad fate. With preparation, planning and the cooperation of company management, your teams can give your company the leading edge in the global marketplace.

This Book Is for You If...

To give you some necessary foundational information, I have included in the first few chapters of this book some background about the development of team culture in the global business community and some predictions about its future as a leadership tool for organizations of all types and sizes. But my main reason for writing this compelling page-turner is not so much to offer a history of teams, but to provide a hands-on, step-by-step how-to guide.

In the following chapters, I have outlined clear and simple steps to help you successfully build a team, set and achieve goals, solve problems and make and implement effective decisions. This book is for you whether you are an executive who wants to introduce the team concept into your organization, a manager responsible for a new team initiative, a team leader (newly appointed or seasoned veteran), or a team member.

This book is also for you if you have been frustrated by previous attempts to tap into the strengths and talents within your organization through teaming for improvement.

I will provide tips and techniques to help you to minimize start-up and implementation problems, deal with growing pains and maximize productivity throughout the life cycle of your improvement teams.

Finally, this book is for you if you're holding on for dear life to the traditional bureaucratic organizational structure that is already going the way of the dinosaur. I understand that you have your own reasons for wanting to cling to the past. Maybe it's comfortable. Maybe you are afraid of making the time, energy and personal commitment to change. Or maybe you just want to avoid facing the opposition you almost certainly will encounter as the harbinger of change. Whatever your reasons, I hope to convince you that teaming is the way of the future. And that the best way to stake your claim to the lion's share of that future is to embrace the team culture now.

To make this book easy to use now and as a reference in the future, I have constructed the progression of the chapters to follow the development of improvement teams from formation through maturation. Even if you are an experienced team leader, I would suggest that you start at the very beginning and read each chapter in sequence. The very least you will gain from this exercise is a good refresher course on teaming for improvement. And who knows? There is always the chance that you could actually stumble upon some valuable new information.

More than just an academic text, this book is a hands-on work tool for you and your team. In order to maximize the usefulness of the text, I have included a small "Workbook Section" after each chapter. Each workbook section is comprised of exercises and other practice components to help team leaders and/or team members put team theory into real-world team practice.

"Key Tips" pages accompanying the main text highlight crucial bits of information and helpful hints. You'll find yourself referring to these key tips time and time again throughout the development of your team.

Of course, all work and no play isn't terribly healthy for anyone. So in addition to the serious stuff, I have included some lighthearted glimpses at today's business world that should give you a chuckle or two. Don't be surprised if you experience a bit of déjà vu when you come across some of these scenarios. Anyone who has been in the business world for any length of time is bound to have come face-to-face with some of the ideologies and situations depicted in this book. Just remember, it's okay to smile, snicker and even laugh out loud. Acknowledging the ludicrous side of a problem can often be the first step toward solving it.

1

MILLENNIUM MODELS

A lot can happen in the course of a thousand years. The changes in all aspects of life are nothing short of monumental. Can you imagine living a thousand years ago? Would you even want to? I am willing to go out on a limb here and say that many of the changes that have occurred since then have been for the best. And many of these profound changes have become so much a part of our daily lives that we rarely think about them.

The new millennium has been getting more hype than any blockbuster movie. It doesn't even need a buzzword or a cute aphorism to introduce it. The new millennium is a fact of life. And it's going to be around for a very long time—one thousand years, to be exact.

But I do know my buzzwords, and I have one to discuss here. That buzzword is "paradigm."

"Paradigm" sounds so educated and elitist, but its meaning is down to earth. A paradigm is a model, pattern or set of principles by which we operate. Paradigms govern the way we live, interact, and work. Paradigms are not set in stone. As the realities of society and the work world change, they change. And when they change, it's called a "paradigm shift."

Take, for example, communications. In the old days—about a decade or so ago—when you had your business cards made up, you included your name, title, company name, mailing address and telephone number. That was the paradigm. Unless your company moved its location or you got promoted, you used those cards until they ran out; then you printed up more.

As we all know, things aren't that simple anymore. First we had to reprint our cards to include a fax number. Not too long after, we had to reprint again to include our company web site and e-mail address. What's next? Who knows...and that's the whole point. One thing we can be sure of, any coming changes will certainly make the printers of business cards happy. If there still are business cards.

The new millennium is a once-in-a-lifetime or once-in-many-lifetimes occasion. The creative wordsmiths of the world have come up with a paradigm to fit the occasion. It's called a "millennium model."

You've heard the expression "the more things change, the more they stay the same." Although that may be comforting to believe, it simply isn't true. And we should all be grateful that it isn't.

Old models are like anchors. They make us feel safe, secure, grounded. The winds of change may be howling around us, but we know we can weather any storm if we just stay put. Sometimes we may wonder if these anchors are holding us back. But we understand them and know how to work with them. They provide us with stability and predictability. After all, it's foolhardy to take risks if you don't have to, isn't it?

Many companies have already recognized the need to cut loose from the anchors of past paradigms and risk avoidance. The names of these companies are often held up as organizational models for the today and for the new millennium. Microsoft. Intel. Federal Express. Each company is known for operating on one key premise—good just isn't good enough.

Early on in their development, these companies realized that the old business paradigms simply didn't apply to the new global marketplace. They knew they had to be willing to surpass their industry standards and create new ones. They knew that, by focusing on future success they had made the commitment to keep on running, even when they could no longer see their competitors way back in the cloud of dust they had left behind.

Those companies were among the first to understand that to fully use their human, information and technology resources, they had to look beyond the traditional top-down organization structure. They quickly learned a valuable secret, the one that *One Minute Manager* and *Gung Ho!* author Kenneth Blanchard calls "The Secret of the Beaver."

When you see a group of beavers repairing a dam that has been hurt by rain, you see there is no real leader. The beavers work together as a team.[1]

Of course, beavers know instinctively what to do with a dam, but it still takes teamwork to ensure that all of the group doesn't simply converge on one section of the dam and wind up fighting about who is going to repair it. They simply work as a team until the dam is fixed. Most humans don't have such a sharply refined set of instincts, especially when it comes to business (except for Bill Gates, Walt Disney, Lee Iacocca and a few other great business minds of this millennium). For most, teaming is not a natural instinct. It is a process that must be learned. And a team leader is essential to that learning process.

There is another major difference between humans and beavers. Humans are subject to shifting paradigms, beavers are not. Think about it. With all due respect for beavers, there is a certain routine procedure to fixing a dam. The beavers collect mud; they collect sticks and they shove the mud and sticks into the damaged sections of the dam. There are no beavers out there trying to build a better dam to impress the other beavers or to entice them to patronize their dam. In other words, the paradigms in beaverdom don't shift a whole lot. At least not as quickly and constantly as they do in the world of business.

Humans need a certain amount of leadership to help them keep track of the rapidly changing paradigms in the global market-place. We also need leaders to help keep the organizational path clear for change by interacting with management, accessing resources and generally removing obstacles.

New Paradigms

No one has a crystal ball. But it really doesn't take a psychic to predict some of the major paradigm shifts that will shape the future of business in the new millennium, not only in the United States but also around the world. Some have already begun to have an impact on how we do business. Others are just out there on the horizon.

Here are five examples of the differences between the old and new millennium models:

Old Model	Millennium Model
Emphasis on Mass Production	Emphasis on Quality and Service
More! More! More!	People Development and Utilization
Assembly Line Mentality	Process Control and Structure from
Process Control and Structure from	On-site
on High	Team-Based Work Systems
Bureaucratic Organizational	
Structure	

Millennium Model Number One: Emphasis on Quality and Service

Sometime in the early 1980s, I recall seeing a television documentary called "If Japan Can, Why Can't We?" The premise of the program intrigued me; its content disturbed me deeply.

Among the business gurus featured in this documentary was a man named Dr. Edward Deming. Although Deming was an American, he was helping the Japanese use quality techniques to upgrade their products. As a result, the Japanese were trouncing their competition—including the Americans—in the global marketplace. You might wonder why Dr. Deming was using his theories and techniques to help Japanese businesses instead of businesses in his own native country.

The plain and simple answer is that American businesses weren't ready to listen to Deming or to anyone else who preached the gospel of quality. Prior to the 1980s, American businesses were too busy making profits in the here and now to think about the future. They were more interested in making a fast dollar than in cultivating long-term relationships with customers. That was the paradigm. In a marketplace free of competition, American industries could call all the shots. They could decide what to manufacture, how much, and what to charge for their goods and services. Mass production was king and, for many companies, customer satisfaction no more than an afterthought.

However, by the early part of that decade, many American companies found themselves with a significant loss of market share in both the domestic and global marketplaces.

Everyone was stunned. What had happened? What secrets had the Japanese discovered that we hadn't?

That television documentary was a revelation to me. But the real wake-up call for American businesses came when the competition from Japan began to take a major toll on their bottom lines. That made many America companies finally sit up and begin to pay attention to the Japanese strategies, methodologies and techniques. They were finally ready to admit that the Japanese were doing something right and that they, themselves, were doing something very wrong.

Unfortunately, even in the light of this startling revelation, some companies never even considered change as an option. They would rather blame the Japanese for stealing their business or the customers for being disloyal than look into their own organizations for answers. Their inflexibility paralyzed them as the paradigms shifted and they didn't. Many of these were quite prominent companies and manufacturing facilities prior to the 1980s. But when the world moved ahead, they stayed behind. Soon, they became extinct.

Fortunately, it wasn't all gloom and doom on the domestic front. Some progressive companies, such as Ford, Motorola and Xerox, did heed the wake-up call. You know their names because they are still alive and thriving as we arrive at the new millennium. They rose to the challenge and turned themselves around by following the Japanese example of incorporating new philosophies and values, and implementing techniques that put quality and teamwork first. Then they went further and added some purely American innovations all their own.

Inspired by these U.S. quality pioneers and convinced by their successes, other companies began to develop a corporate culture based on a quality first philosophy. To develop and implement the improvement strategies necessary for shifting to a customer-oriented mode, many introduced teams into their organizational structure. For those companies, the rewards have been far-reaching and highly visible. In addition to a stronger bottom line, some have earned the U.S. Department of Commerce's national Malcolm Baldridge Award. Others have participated in team competitions sponsored by such national quality organizations as the Association of Quality and Participation (AQP). But the most important prizes they have earned have been the trust, respect and continued patronage of customers in the global marketplace.

That doesn't mean that the heated competition is over. In fact, it's only just shifting into high gear. So now is certainly not the time for American business to rest on its laurels. Remember, we're not the only ones who learned the secrets of the Japanese and took them to heart.

Sweeping changes are happening every day. Technologies are changing. Economics is changing. The configurations of nations are changing. Customer needs are changing. In light of all this change, all institutions, whether in the public or private sector, must remain committed to improvement through radical reengineering or through continuous improvement efforts.

In my professional consulting capacity, I see a growing number of companies shifting from organizations with several levels of management to matrix- and team-based structures utilizing empowered and flexible self-directed teams. Why? Because these companies are discovering that teams are better able to respond to changes in the marketplace. Even more important, when teams are really working up to speed, they are often able to anticipate changes before they occur.

Take the reengineering and redesign teams at the financial subsidiary of a major telecommunications firm. This company achieved a 33 percent increase in customer satisfaction, a fivefold increase in profits over the last five years, and a working environment for employees that is regarded as one of the best in the industry. Quite an accomplishment! How did they manage it? With the guidance and support of an enlightened leader, Tom Wajnert, the company made a full-scale commitment to quality, spending several months redesigning the way work is done, using teams and discarding antiquated department structures that resulted in delay, rework and retarded workflow.

We also now see organizations such as GE adopting teams and improvement strategies that were once confined to their manufacturing operations, and applying them to their financial subsidiaries within the GE capital unit. The unit's goal is clearly defined—to surpass the performance of competitive financial services by attaining the challenging goal of only three defects per million. As I write this book, the company is well on its way toward achieving that goal.

I don't want you to think I'm minimizing the challenges of reconfiguring organization's structure. But my research and personal experience have convinced me that any company can change paradigms, views and practices provided that management is wholeheartedly on board. Management must acknowledge that teaming is to be incorporated as a fundamental part of the business, rather than used as a quick fix for quality or service emergencies.

Every single person in the organization, from the CEO to the workers on the front line, must adopt the mindset and practices that place quality first. Sounds logical. After all, who could argue against quality? Actually, the answer may surprise you (or if you have already encountered resistance to improvement strategies, you probably won't be surprised at all). Many times the strongest opposition doesn't come from the employees on the front line, the ones who put the strategies into practice. Often the organization's senior leadership erects the most challenging obstacles and the highest brick walls. Why? Because a non-bureaucratic structure allows the front line employee, the one closest to the customers, to do more decision making for the business. With that responsibility comes the chance to gain company-wide respect and recognition. And that can be a threatening prospect for a bureaucrat. That's why it takes a truly enlightened leader to be an advocate of employee empowerment and teaming. But that's another book altogether....

Here are some of the elements that every company doing business in the new millennium will have to incorporate into every department of its organization and ingrain into every fiber of its corporate culture:

- The customer defines quality and service. Everyone must be aware of this fact and respond to customer desires and needs as they change.
- Improving quality and service requires improving the processes that produce them. These improvements must be made on a continuous basis.
- Quality and service do not necessarily cost more, and may cost less if approached in the most efficient way.
- Quality and service levels must be measured in order to be improved.
- Higher levels of quality and service are achieved by focusing on the way in which work is performed on a daily basis, as well as working on future improvements.

The organizations I have mentioned so far in this chapter have embraced many or even all of these elements. In fact, a number of these organizations have incorporated the elements into their overall operating principals, the set of values that serve as conduct guidelines for all organization members, including management.

Savvy organizations realize that it's not enough to ask individual workers to review and adjust their own work processes based on the most current set of operating principals. While that is an important first step, their individual efforts must be supported by the efforts of continuous improvement teams and larger redesign or reengineering teams to define, design and implement changes in the basic structure, systems and workflow of the organization. Only with this kind of mutual internal support can a company hope to achieve truly significant improvements in quality and service.

Millennium Model Number Two: More with Less

Before the 1980s, corporate sprawl was a sign of success. Big meant powerful. Compact meant "You've still got a long way to go before you'll be able to play with the big guys."

Today, the opposite is true. Sprawl is cumbersome, unfocused and wasteful. Compact is "lean and mean," quick, ready to pounce on an opportunity. Compact companies have always had to make the most of all of their resources, human, material and technological. They were never in any position to become lazy, fat and happy. They were always hungry and always looking for ways to maximize their limited resources. Because they had to rely more on innovative thinking and focused implementation, these companies were often able to make more of their resources than many of the larger companies with virtually unlimited resources.

When I say "compact," I don't necessarily mean "small." A company can have many departments and subsidiaries scattered around the country and across the globe, yet be lean, agile and hungry. It depends upon how their resources are structured, managed and utilized.

Compact companies have learned a valuable lesson, one that will take them far in the new millennium. They have learned that less can actually be more. And, with the increased global competition and rapid depletion of resources in today's marketplace, less is what most companies have to work with.

Now that's not to say that, even for sprawling companies, wholesale organization-wide head-chopping is the answer. That's a lot like cutting off your arms and legs to lose weight. A number of companies did try it, though. They're the ones who gave restructuring a bad reputation. Most of the time these companies were left not with a lean, agile organization, but with a flimsy skeleton. Upset by the random ravaging, good people would get busy hunting for other jobs. Drones would hide out, hoping to be overlooked in the massacre. And management would be focused on how many salaries they could trim from the budget, rather than making the improvements that would get the company on the right track.

The good news is that it is possible for companies to "lose the fat" that has been making them sluggish and unable to compete without lopping off any important appendages. Here are four steps that can go a long way toward helping organizations maximize their resources:

- Adopt continuous improvement to achieve greater results with the resources available.
- Prioritize and focus the human, financial and physical resources of the organization on those things that will bring the greatest return.
- Ensure that everyone in the organization is pulling consistently in the same direction.
- Develop the knowledge, skills and capabilities of all people to perform a broader range of functions and make greater contributions.

Recognize that everyone will have to work harder at times just to keep the organization in the race. Not always a pleasant prospect, I know. Everyone thinks that he or she works hard enough. So it is crucial that everyone understands and accepts the fact that this is a necessary phase in the development in the company and that the resulting changes will benefit them personally as well as the company as a whole. As a manager, be sure to demonstrate that you are willing to work harder, too. Getting in with the crew and pulling the oars can go a long way toward proving to them that you are as committed to the changes as you expect them to be.

Most American businesses have a bureaucratic structure. And although that structure may have many levels, it actually has only two major strata—management and everyone else. Management develops the policies, makes the important decisions, calls the shots. Everyone else does what management tells them to do. The "everyone else" group includes those who perform the actual work. If management needs a little extra high-level support, consultants are called in. You can't argue that this structure is straightforward. And, too bad it doesn't work.

This structure is based on the assumption that the "everyone else" group has nothing to contribute to the decision-making process. The group's intellect, ingenuity and insights go unacknowledged for the most part, and untapped.

Today a growing number of organizations are discovering that they can no longer afford to support a two-strata structure. They are no longer able to rely solely on managers and outside experts to make all the decisions and implement all the improvements

I don't want to cause panic among all the managers out there. There will certainly always be a need for managers and experts. They will continue to play key roles, but those roles will change. More responsibility for routine management will be absorbed by the people performing the work, who are closer to the front lines, where the action is and the decisions must be made. The people who do the work will be accountable for their decisions and they will own the processes in which they are involved. They will still require the guidance of leaders, but they will be expected to actively identify problems and find solutions rather than wait around for someone higher up to tell them what to do.

Successful organizations in the future will continually expand the capabilities and responsibilities of their employees. Some of my client companies have even symbolically done away with the term "employees," instead referring to them as "associates" or "members" to encourage their active participation in the improvement of the company.

A pharmaceutical firm for which I recently performed some improvement facilitation reengineered the work processes throughout its entire computer servicing operation. Managers had to learn to go from being sole decision-makers to facilitators, offering guidance, support and assistance to the company's newborn teams. Individual workers and team members had to learn to become process owners, responsible for making more decisions in their designated process areas, and accountable for the results of those decisions. People from all departments and disciplines throughout the company had to learn to work together in cross-functional teams.

Another pharmaceutical company has used teams to reduce new product development time by 30 percent. This allows new drugs to be brought to market in record time.

Rhone-Poulenc Rorer (RPR), one of the top fifteen pharmaceutical companies in the world, is exemplary in the creative use of teams.

Three of the company's primary objectives are to develop new drugs, to manufacture them quickly and to get them to market immediately. Being a progressive company, RPR recognized that teaming would improve performance in all three areas. Because RPR is an international company, it had a unique set of needs. Any given project might involve a chemist in Paris, a staff expert in Japan, and a marketing manager in Pennsylvania, or some other configuration of company personnel at various points around the globe. It certainly would not be feasible to bring these people together physically in a single location for regular meetings. But today's technologies offer other options such as e-mail, computer conferencing, videoconferencing, etc. Now RPR has a number of "virtual teams" that use these technologies to bring key personnel together wherever they may be based at any time.[2]

Although acquisition of communication devices, training and other resources may be necessary for virtual teams and some other technology-based contemporary team structures, the time and money spent in development is well worth it. These teams show that with a little innovation and a lot of commitment, companies can find ways to use all their resources—particularly their human resources—to their fullest potential. The results these teams have achieved are clear evidence that today's companies can indeed accomplish more with less.

Millennium Model Number Three: People Development and Utilization

I have been a facilitator of management development programs for a number of years. In that time, I have seen many changes—and I have had to incorporate them into my training sessions. Never a dull moment! Even a facilitator never has this management stuff down cold. We have to shift with the paradigms like everyone else.

For example, not so many years ago, one of the major leadership characteristics emphasized for management personnel was "control." "Control" meant managerial monitoring and follow-up to ensure that work and projects were proceeding according to plan. However, some managers interpreted this as a directive to command, to take charge, stand tough and get those troops to shape up. It meant that the manager always had to be in control of his or her people, resources, processes, outcomes.

It was all part of the vertical organizational structure, a structure that was modeled after the military hierarchy. I even heard of one manager who was so taken with the military-inspired structure that he used to tell his "troops" to "always remember that I am the gun and you are only the ammunition." Translation: You give your ideas to me and I'll take them upstairs so I can take credit for them. Not exactly the greatest inspirational leader I ever heard of. Not surprisingly, many of his prized bullets turned on him and left the company for a less stifling environment.

This Napoleonic manager aside, leaders have traditionally had to try to live up to some pretty burdensome and often unrealistic expectations. Leadership was a lonely job. It was a job filled with stress. You couldn't turn to your supervisor for guidance because that might be viewed as a sign of weakness. You couldn't turn to your employees for help because the boss was always expected to have the answers and to be in complete control. No wonder so many managers were constantly nervous, irritable and even paranoid.

What a difference a decade or two can make! Today's teams have removed many of the constraints from leader-employee relationships. If more people are intimately involved in making decisions about a process, more people feel inclined and empowered to take ownership of it. Instead of pounding their heads against the wall trying to constantly come up with all the ideas and innovations, managers can now play a more powerful role by cultivating the participation and creativity of others. This win-win situation gives everyone involved increased motivation, inspiration and pride in a job well done.

We see how teams benefit managers in an organization. But that's only part of the story. The team setting also provides team members with opportunities for growth and learning. Great, right?

Well, it certainly can be. But (here's another of my famous caveats) all those wonderful opportunities are likely to go to waste if the individuals who make up the teams are not prepared to take advantage of them. Without sufficient "people development," teams become not a source of inspiration, but one of frustration and disillusionment. By neglecting to prepare people for the challenges of teaming, many companies have doomed their team efforts to failure from the very beginning.

However, progressive companies that recognize that the first step toward successful team development is intensive *people* development can ensure a more positive outcome for their teams. One of the business units of a major telecommunications company actually designed a team for the express purpose of implementing training for the many new process improvement teams forming throughout the organization. This insightful move helped the unit make a smoother transition from traditional to team culture. It also paved the way for the eventual evolution to self-directed teams.

At a small manufacturing firm in Pennsylvania, the senior leader made it a priority to provide team leader and team member training before initiating a number of process improvement initiatives. He also provided the members of his own staff with leadership development training so they could better support the efforts of the teams. With a solid foundation of people development, the teams were able to minimize many of the usual start-up problems and get right down to business: the business of quality improvement.

Millennium Model Number Four: Process Control and Structure

There's that word "control" again. Only now it has a very different connotation.

Instead of people control, the emphasis has turned to *process* control. And it involves not a single beleaguered leader, but the organization as a whole.

As I explained before, the organization structure that will prevail in the new millennium is not the traditional dictatorship. It is an entirely new kind of structure based on mutual trust and respect between company management and team members. This structure relies on people and teams to manage their own activities and the processes for which they are responsible. Consistent with this philosophy, employees define the necessary controls to monitor and improve their processes. In addition, they establish their own measurements and goals to monitor and improve the performance of the areas for which they are responsible. This is a shift from a results-only orientation to a process orientation that places equal emphasis on the means by which results are achieved.

In 1995, Rochester General Hospital in New York introduced a team-centered initiative. Doctors and nurses at the hospital rarely speak to one another during cardiac surgery. Are they feuding? Hardly. Four years ago, the hospital charged its cardiac surgery team with the task of reengineering the way it operates (no pun intended) to the point at which everything—from the way anesthesia is administered to the way tools and towels are stacked—is standardized. As a result, the team cut steps that wasted time and energy, making surgery time shorter and more efficient. These moves have also significantly enhanced patient health (fewer problems after surgery, better chance of survival) and reduced health care costs.

Rochester General Hospital has been so successful in its incorporation of teams that it has become a model for other hospitals. In fact, the hospital has been such a stellar example for the industry that it was announced in *USA Today* on May 1 that the hospital had been awarded the 1998 RIT/USA Today Quality Cup for health care excellence.[3]

We've already seen how teams have helped break down the barriers between the upper management strata and the lower everyone-else strata. But, as the Rochester General Hospital case history shows, teaming also goes a long way in breaking through the bureaucratic layers that defined the traditional vertical organizational structure.

Until recently, these rigid layers have served as brick walls, blocking the flow of communication and information, and frustrating initiative. Instead of facilitating cooperative effort, the traditional structure isolated people and functions. Work wasn't shared; it was "handed off" from one department or bureaucratic level to another. For people in many companies, the walls were so thick they were almost visible. That's why another popular term for handing off in such functionally structured companies is "tossing it over the wall."

This "I've done my part, now it's your problem" mentality has often led to costly variances in workflow and a greater potential for errors. It has also led to a lot of finger-pointing when something goes wrong. Often the work was viewed as a virtual hot potato being passed back and forth. In many cases, departments or individuals would toss the work back, sending it back for rework, because the previous group's efforts didn't meet their requirements or come up to their standards. One thing was for sure, no one wanted to be caught with the hot potato when the music stopped and accountability was involved.

When things went terribly wrong, everyone spent more time, energy and ingenuity in finding ways to point the finger at someone else than in solving the problem. Of course, the big loser was the customer. Their needs were changing, but everyone within the organization was too busy bickering and covering their backs to acknowledge, let alone respond to, those changing needs.

In their ultimate incarnations, teams can eliminate the need for all this nonsense. With increased communication, cooperation and process quality accountability, teams are attuned to the changing needs of their customers. Therefore, they are able to respond quickly, efficiently and accurately to meet those needs.

In a telecommunications business unit, I facilitated a redesign team formed to investigate all the errors and workflow problems caused by work hand-offs. They redesigned the structure of the organization into self-directed teams, each accountable for its own critical core processes. Each team was structured to minimize hand-offs and non-value-added activities in their workflow processes. Using carefully designed customer and financial measures, the company has achieved significant improvement in productivity, profitability and customer satisfaction.

We have clearly established that the traditional vertical organizational structure is dysfunctional. We know that teams provide a viable solution. That has been proven when natural teams of people accountable to a specific manager and sharing designated outputs work together to complete regular, ongoing work responsibilities. Often these teams are referred to as departments, but they are still examples of teaming at its most basic level. There have also been ad hoc SWAT teams designed for quick action and response to immediate problems and issues.

Today, companies are coming up with more and more innovative and effective approaches to using team structures for improvement. The four major improvement team approaches are:

The Continuous Improvement Approach

This most basic approach involves commissioning teams on an ad hoc basis to review:

- Critical customer requirements—this applies to both internal customers (other teams, management, fellow team members, etc.) and external customers
- Internal processes for differentiating value-added from non-value-added steps.

Using the data collected from these reviews, the team should then be able to suggest solutions for continuous improvement.

Of course, this approach can only work if team leader and members are trained to recognize changing customer requirements, understand who all of their customers are, and tell the difference between value-added and non-value-added steps and solutions.

In many of my client organizations, the teams that are created to work on improvements are cross-functional. While they may not manage specific processes, they often contribute to significant improvement since they can identify hand-offs and resulting errors between functions that may have been holding the company's progress back for years. By enabling these problem areas to be identified and any issues addressed and resolved, the cross-functional continuous improvement approach can make a significant reduction in work redundancy, errors, resource waste and money spent.

The Project Approach

Projects associated with major undertakings for the organization are often assigned to specific teams. These projects may include a new product launch, a move to another work location within the same building or a brand-new facility, introduction of new products or policies, etc. Depending upon the nature and complexity of the projects, the team may be functional (having members drawn from a single business function) or cross-functional (bringing people from various disciplines within the organization together to manage a particular process or project across functions). Relatively simple projects, such as moving to a new work location within some building, may require a functional team to work together for only a month or two. More complex projects may require a cross-functional team to work together for a much longer period of time. For example, the launching of a new product into the marketplace may require a team composed of product development, production, marketing and sales personnel. Some companies (such as the Rhone-Poulenc Rorer example mentioned earlier) are beginning to form virtual teams to enable them to call in the skills, experience and insights of members all over the world.

In the earliest stages of introducing this approach into an organization, it is not uncommon for some conflict and confusion to arise. But be patient. Over time, these "birth pangs" will ease and any problems can be resolved.

The Self-Directed (Self-Managed) Team Approach

Traditionally, individuals were designated "leaders." Today, in many organizations, the word "leader" is also applied to teams.

Over time, some teams are able to evolve to the point at which they actually operate as small business units. Members make their own assignments, select additional team members and perform other important assignments such as peer review, preparing budgets and hiring and firing.

This doesn't mean that these teams work in isolation, as independent sovereign entities separate from the rest of the organization. It simply means they have truly taken control of the processes, areas or objectives for which they are responsible. It means they can manage their own work activities and always be prepared to quickly recognize and respond to the need for change.

Can self-directed teams really work? A recent study of more than one thousand employees of a telecommunications company that had developed self-managing teams in a variety of functions over several years suggests that they certainly can—and do. The study concludes that self-managed teams are significantly more effective in improving quality of work life and productivity than are comparable traditionally managed groups that perform the same customer service, technical support and administrative functions. According to the study, ratings of performance by both team members and higher level managers were higher for self-managing teams.[4]

The Process Reengineering Approach

When an organization uses this approach, it is clear that there is a deep commitment to change. This is the "big guns" approach, the one that can turn an organization on its head. For this type of team, incremental improvement isn't enough. Process reengineering teams work toward making radical changes in the critical core processes of their company's business and, in some cases, actually redesigning the organization itself.

In this scenario, a design team or reengineering team commissioned by a steering committee creates and often implements major designs that bring about radical change and improvement. Sometimes, larger-scale design efforts require employees from all over the company to work with the team.

Typically, design teams or reengineering teams focus on the big picture, mapping ideal processes and determining how to combine technology and self-directed teams to attain these ideals. Needless to say, this approach requires the most radical changes in behaviors and skills on the part of the entire organization. So, although this approach can provide the greatest opportunities for communication, efficiency and responsiveness to changing customer needs and marketplace conditions, don't expect miracles overnight. Depending on the levels of teaming skills and commitment among members of the organization, change will probably occur at an evolutionary rather than a revolutionary pace. As these skill and commitment levels grow, groups that begin life as managed teams may progress to self-managed teams within a relatively brief period of time, if there is patience, support and assistance from upper management.

The following example emphasizes the crucial role of consistent leadership support for design and reengineering teams during the design phase of their work as well as during implementation. In this example, the team took more than eight months to arrive at a final design and implementation plan. At first thought, this probably seems like a very long time to tie up a key group of people in a company. But management was patient, and ultimately that patience paid off.

Because the team was given the time it needed for detailed analysis of and careful reflection on the organization's current situation, future needs and possible solutions, the radical changes the team finally proposed were accepted and successfully piloted. What makes this situation particularly noteworthy is the fact that many of the changes were monumental. Yet the transitions were smooth, and the long-term impact on the business, on the internal structure and the bottom line, was positive.

One of the most important contributions the company's management provided throughout this effort was to clear the path for a company-wide communications flow. This allowed the team members to obtain all the information they needed to make sound decisions. It also helped to alleviate the resistance, ranging from mild to rabid, with which most people respond to change.

It's no revelation that people tend to fear most the things they least understand. In business, the thing that people usually fear most and understand least is change. Without open communications, people in an organization may regard a team's efforts as interference, meddling in a system that they believe works just fine. They may feel threatened that the team's findings and recommendations may result in more work for them, reduction in job status or even elimination of their positions. And the more time they have to sit and stew about it (for example, the eight months it took the redesign team to announce its conclusions), the more hostile and less productive they are likely to become.

A sound system of communication enables everyone to feel that they are in the loop every step of the way. More facts mean less conjecture, fewer rumors, less resentment and panic. Communication allows everyone within the organization to participate in the process and outcome of the team's efforts. It allows people throughout the company to recognize their role as participants in—rather than as victims of—the process of change.

Millennium Model Number Five: Team-Based Work Systems

In the early days of our history, most work was done by individual craftsmen who performed all tasks associated with the making and, often, the marketing of a product. In the early days of the Industrial Revolution, tasks were broken down into segments and workers performed their segments of the task on an individual basis. In the global economy of the new millennium, the complex nature of products and services will require increased interaction among people and coordination of individual and group efforts. It will require the development of a greater number and variety of teams.

As a nation, we take great pride in and attribute much of our greatness to rugged individualism and entrepreneurial courage. We tend to forget that our most impressive achievements were made by people working together linked by a common vision, commitment and objectives.

No single individual could have tamed this country's great rivers, won World War II or conquered killer diseases. I am among those who recall vividly how, in 1957, the United States was caught napping when the Soviet Union suddenly kicked the space race into high gear with the successful launch of a satellite named Sputnik. Americans were horrified that another country had been able to beat us, the greatest of all world powers (in our estimation anyway), to the punch. Many were more than a little frightened about how this stunning Soviet achievement might affect the long-term global balance of power.

It took people with foresight, such as presidents Dwight D.

Eisenhower and John F. Kennedy, to turn that growing panic into determination to regain the position of leadership. President Eisenhower quickly signed into being two government agencies created specifically to get us back on the right road. One was the National Aeronautics and Space Administration (NASA). The other was a division of the Department of Defense called the Advanced Research Projects Administration (currently known as the Defense Advanced Research Project Agency).

While John Kennedy was president, he initiated the Apollo manned space exploration program. And in 1969, Apollo 11 made world history when an American astronaut named Neil Armstrong became the first human being to walk on the moon.

Of course, we know that even the greatest of leaders couldn't possibly have achieved anything of that magnitude without help. This is where both presidents showed their real visionary abilities. They knew that, in order for their space programs to be effective, they would have to cultivate nationwide support for them. That meant gaining commitment for the programs from a wide range of publics including Congress, the scientific community and the American people. It would even take a lot of hard work to gain consensus among the scientists and officials from the space programs themselves. But these presidents understood these challenges and they successfully overcame them. And the rest, as they say, is history.

Perhaps retail magnate Sam Walton said it best when he stated, "Individuals don't win; teams do." Although Walton has long been acknowledged as the epitome of the successful entrepreneur, he describes the phenomenon of Wal-Mart as simply "a spectacular example of what happens when people find a way to work together...to put their individual egos behind the needs of the team."[5]

The sports world is filled with examples of great teams without great players and poor teams with great players. They are clear examples of how a balance of individual capability and responsibility coupled with team effort and cooperation is what produces great teams and great results.

General Electric (GE) Mortgage Insurance really put its

commitment to improvement to the acid test when it pulled ten of its most successful representatives ("reps") off their regular jobs and designated them to a team for ten months. The reason? Because if ten great reps could make an impact on the company, think how much greater that impact would be if there was a whole company full of reps with the same skill levels and decision-making abilities! It was a mind-boggling prospect, and a somewhat risky project, but it made perfect sense to the progressive management at GE.

The team's mission was to develop a program that would enable other reps to pass along the secrets that enabled them to balance customer needs with business realities. This team's members had a consistently high record of accurately predicting which home buyers who were delinquent in their mortgage payments would eventually be able to recover and make good on their payments, and which were less likely to do so.

Since its implementation, the program developed by the team of master reps has resulted in a near-perfect record of predicting efficiently and effectively which way mortgage default situations should be handled. The program wound up saving GE about $8 million. Because the program shows reps how to achieve results without needlessly hassling customers, customer satisfaction ratings have also risen from 61 percent to 76 percent. In an article in *USA Today* of May 1, 1998, announcing the selection of GE Mortgage Insurance as winner of its RIT/USA Quality Cup for the services industry, one of the competition judges explained that one of the things that impressed him most was "an amazing executive involvement" throughout the eight months of development of the program and its implementation."[6]

Team-Based Work System Development

A team is a group of people, but that doesn't mean every group is a team. Work groups exist wherever a job takes more than one person to complete. Typically, the common links in a work group are the supervisor, function, equipment and location. Members of a traditional work group usually tend to perform their work individually and to be accountable for their individual performance and results.

Even professions that are commonly believed to require a high degree of independent functioning (such as research scientists, lawyers, truck drivers, and others) are turning to teamwork to keep up with technological advances and the increasingly complex nature of their jobs. But this move toward teaming doesn't in any way minimize the value or importance of the individual. Quite the contrary. This team orientation can:

- Lead to greater individual responsibility, greater creativity, increased flexibility, better decisions, faster responses and higher performance
- Provide the best way for the people closest to the process and customers to take responsibility for the needs of the customers
- Contribute substantially to greater job satisfaction, enhanced self-esteem, a sense of value and better work relationships

When I am facilitating programs for team leaders or members, I like to use something called the "Subarctic Survival Exercise" to bring home the benefits of teaming.[7] Participants are asked to imagine that they are all survivors of a plane crash. After being given a list of items that have also made it through the crash, each participant is told to rank the items in order of importance to his or her survival.

Once the ranking is completed by each individual, the team is asked to rank the items once again, this time using the process of consensus decision making rather than individual judgment. The differences in the rankings are often remarkable and quite surprising to the program participants. Even those who showed careful thought and intelligence in their rankings often find that consensual decision making in a team setting produces the most logical, creative, practical and, ultimately, workable conclusions.

I like this exercise because it puts some important theories about teaming into real-life terms. Team leaders and members have a chance to practice high-performance behaviors in a high-commitment setting. (And what could be a higher commitment than survival?) This exercise also clearly illustrates the truth in the words "the whole is greater than the sum of its parts."

Characteristics and Functions of Team-Based Work Systems

Some or all of the following characteristics can define team-based work systems:

- Everyone is a member of a team, each team is a part of a larger team and all teams are part of the greater organizational team.
- Leadership can come from within the team as well as from outside the team, and leadership roles can shift as the team matures and develops.
- The team leader can be a team member (or several members), or a supervisor whose responsibilities have been refined.

Most teams are organized around business processes or products and services. However, one of the companies most committed to customer service I have worked with was one that also had teams organized around geography. This East Coast-based company had one customer service team that worked on East Coast time, meaning that they would work during regular East Coast business hours. To make certain that clients on the West Coast were equally well served, the company also had a second team that would arrive later in the day and stay well into the evenings. For this company, the East Coast-West Coast time difference made no difference in its commitment to customer service.

- Teams have a clear understanding and knowledge of customers and their requirements.
- Teams are guided and linked by a common business vision, set of principles, mission and outcome focus.
- Team member responsibilities tend to grow as the team members develop and self-management tends to evolve.

As I noted, there are many different types of teams. Depending on the type and specific needs of an organization, team functions and responsibilities may include any or all of the following:

- Perform the work necessary to produce the products and services for which the team is responsible.

- Manage the team's own work activities, including planning and scheduling, budgeting, quality and safety.
- Make decisions as necessary within the team's area of responsibility.
- Manage performance by setting goals, measuring progress and taking appropriate corrective action.
- Identify, analyze, develop and implement improvement.
- Communicate and share information, knowledge and skills both inside and outside the team as necessary to perform the team's mission and serve its customers.

Summing Up

As we move into the next century and toward a global economy, the work environment looks, feels and behaves differently. No one can stop the constant acceleration of change. Therefore, organizations have only two choices: adapt or die. It is that simple and that dire. Flexibility, anticipation and responsiveness are the characteristics that will identify successful companies. Rigidity, complacency and stagnation will be the characteristics of those destined to fail.

It is a certainty that teams will be an important and powerful tool for improvement into the next millennium. In many companies, teams have already begun to replace antiquated organizational structures in the quest for continuous and radical improvement.

In most companies, teams require a major cultural shift, not simply in structure, but in the mindsets of everyone within the organization. They require unequivocal support from all levels of leadership and unimpeded company wide communication, understanding, cooperation and commitment. Teaming is an evolutionary process. It takes a great deal of patience from everyone involved. But the time and effort devoted to the transition to a team culture now may be the salvation of American business in the very near future. In fact, during the latter part of this decade, we have begun to experience the impact of teaming and to acknowledge its importance.

Workbook Section

Practice Exercises

TEAM LEADERS

Review and discuss the implications that each of the five Millennium Models has for your team members and for others outside your team.

Facilitate a discussion of the approach your team is taking (continuous improvement, cross-functional, self-managed, reengineering, combination)? What does this mean in terms of the methodologies and communication plans you may use?

TEAM MEMBERS

1. Find your team's direction. Take five minutes for each team member to brainstorm a list of ideas to identify your team's purpose, its reason for existing. Short phrases on post-it notes are easier to use than long, wordy lists. Use a whiteboard to record group responses. Consolidate ideas based on redundancies. Group like ideas together.

2. Changing business conditions will create workplace changes. Looking ahead, identify three external changes you think will have a positive impact on your workplace and three that you are concerned about. What impact will these changes have on what you do or how you operate as a team? Discuss.

Positive Changes

_____

_____

_____

Causes for Concern

_____

_____

_____

Key Tips

If you are just forming a team or have been together for some time, clarify which of the four major approaches your team will be adopting.

Make sure you have reviewed and discussed the Millennium Models as a team. Key questions and actions you might consider (depending on how long you have been together) include:

- How will you emphasize quality and service?
- Have you been (or will you be) considering how to achieve "more with less"?
- How will you develop, as team members, to make full use of each individual's strengths?
- Have you thought about ideas concerning process control and structure?

Discuss

- What resistance might you encounter as your organization moves toward team-based work systems? What resources or assistance might you need to deal with this resistance?

If You Don't Know Where You're Going,
Any Road Will Do!

2

TEAM DIRECTION

In one plant operation, a team improved packaging to the point at which the company was able to significantly decrease equipment purchasing costs and reduce overtime expenses four-teenfold.

In his book, *The Seven Habits of Highly Effective People,* author Stephen Covey notes that one reason these people are so effective and successful is that they always "Begin With The End in Mind"™.[1] In other words, they find out where they're going before they even begin to try to figure out how to get there. Obvious? Well, it should be. But all too often people are so anxious to get off the starting blocks that they neglect to get a good fix on the finish line. They can run hard and run fast, but where they'll end up is anyone's guess.

My experience with the development of improvement teams—no matter which approach they take—confirms this conclusion time and time again. It is a fact that the teams that "begin with an end in mind" are more likely to achieve a high performance level much quicker and are less likely to engage in the kinds of major conflict that can really bog down the team's ability to progress, particularly during the early stages of team development.

That's why the first step for any team must be to develop a charter. While details may vary according to the improvement approach the team adopts, all charters share four common elements: a vision, a mission, principles and goals.

When you first become a member of a team, it is natural to feel a little anxious, somewhat apprehensive, perhaps even ill at ease. If you're like me, some of the questions you are probably asking yourself may include:

- Will I like this team?
- Will the other members like me?
- What are we supposed to do?
- How are we going to get things done?
- What are the do's and don'ts around here?

All quite logical questions...none of which will probably have an immediate answer. However, the charter development sessions are a good place to start.

As team members voice their opinions, insights and ideas during these sessions, individual personalities begin to emerge. Sometimes personalities will clash. In those cases, the early sessions are a good time to work on improving personal interaction skills and practice conflict resolution.

The exercise of developing a charter can also offer quite a revealing preview of how the giant jigsaw puzzle that is every team will eventually look and function when all of the pieces are fitted together properly.

Four Key Elements of the Charter

Back to the four key elements of the charter. Unless they are clearly defined at the outset, they can become a source of confusion rather than of clarity. For example, people often confuse the vision with the mission and the goals. To make them easy to keep straight, here are some simple ways to differentiate these elements:

Vision is a picture of the future. It is an overall image of what the organization wants to become, to be known for or to achieve. It tends to be general in nature so it can capture the attention of and be easily understood by everyone inside and outside the organization.

A good example is the vision that prevails in one of the companies with which I have worked. That vision is "The Simply Better Healthcare Company." It's brief, to the point, general in nature, yet communicates a long-term set of initiatives. Most important of all, it is frequently and powerfully articulated by the company's leadership throughout the organization.

Mission defines the organization's purpose, its competitive edge and its key accomplishments that will be necessary to bring the vision to life. The mission of the Starship *Enterprise* in the TV show *Star Trek,* for example, is to explore new worlds and boldly go where no one has gone before. Another familiar statement, "Quality is Job One," clearly defined the mission of Ford for a number of years. These catchy little statements are called mission statements.

What can happen if the mission is missing…if there is no single defining thought to bring it all together for everyone within the organization? As we discussed earlier, in 1962, President John F. Kennedy challenged NASA and the nation to put a man on the moon by the end of the decade. This was a clear and compelling mission prompted by the fiercely competitive spirit and achievements of the Soviet Union. The outcome? In the words of Apollo 11 astronaut Neil Armstrong, "One small step for a man; one giant leap for mankind."

In the 1990s, however, NASA has no clear, compelling vision. As a result, it is struggling, constantly battling for funds, unable to generate enthusiasm among government officials or the general public, and, quite simply, not quite certain what the future will—or should—hold.

Just as every organization should have a mission statement, so should every team. While it may take the team a session or two or sometimes even more to agree to an overall purpose, the investment in time early in the life of the team can go a long way toward building consensus and commitment among team members. And, as I explained before, the earlier that happens, the better for everyone.

Some leaders and members are dismayed when immediate consensus is not quickly or easily reached. But, from what I have seen in organizations, that's a good rather than a bad omen for the team's future success. It shows that the members are already thinking and are ready to communicate with one another. The last thing you want in a team is a bunch of "yes men or women." You want a group of people who are innovative and who will not hesitate to challenge one another. So what if it gets a little loud sometimes? Chalk it up to enthusiasm, unless the punches start flying. That is definitely a team no-no.

It may be helpful for a steering committee or sponsor to offer the team guidelines and objectives for developing its mission. When bringing together a group of people with diverse interests, skills and backgrounds, it is a good idea to provide a common starting point.

Guiding principles are the do's and don'ts of team behavior. They are the broad values and beliefs people use in performing their work, making decisions and relating to people within and outside the work unit. Guiding principles help to define and shape the culture for achieving the mission and vision.

Many consider the Ten Commandments to be the most important guiding principles in their lives. The Constitution outlines the principles that guide the United States.

Two principles that I regularly encounter working with improvement-oriented organizations include:
- We will treat people with dignity and respect.
- We will be flexible and nimble with customers.

Teams usually base their principles on those used to guide the organization as a whole. Many of these principles define the accepted overall conduct of the team and its members. Others are specifically associated with the team's work and meeting behaviors (e.g., one conversation at a time; team members will work to complete assignments between meetings). I have seen some teams that are so adamant about the timeliness of their meetings that they penalize team members who show up late with a one-dollar fine for each minute they are late. I have always thought that was one of the more painful ways to enforce a guiding principle.

It is important that these principles be used merely as guides and not set in concrete (except, of course, for the ones that call for common courtesy and respect for others). The more effective teams will visit these principles from time to time to validate their appropriateness and monitor team behavior at different stages of the team's existence.

Goals are the milestones you achieve along the way to accomplish the mission. They are very specific and, depending upon the approach under which the team is operating, they can range from widely comprehensive to narrowly defined. For example, a process improvement team may set as one of its goals the reduction of cycle time by 20 percent or the reduction in the number of defects by 10 percent. On the other hand, a reengineering team may set as its goal a 50 percent or more improvement in core business processes.

While setting major goals early in a team's development is important for establishing a direction for its efforts, the team must be prepared to adjust those goals as they encounter new information and circumstances along the way. Ad hoc improvement teams in particular must be flexible in their goal-setting as their review of customer requirements and process problems uncovers rework and other forms of non-value-added time and waste that must be dealt with.

In a recent Association for Quality and Participation (AQP) Team Competition, Daishowa America's TGWANUY (Thank Goodness We Are Not Unemployed Yet) Team presented examples of its goals and achievements. Daishowa America manufactures telephone directory paper and operates a wood chip import/export facility adjacent to the paper mill. Daishowa America is owned by Daishowa North America Corp., Ltd. and is located in Port Angeles, Washington in the corner of the Pacific Northwest.

TGWANUY, a Daishowa Team Concept (DTC) team redesigned, fabricated and installed an upgraded barker outfeed system (equipment that strips bark from logs prior to sending the log through the chipper). With the implementation of their project, the 1997 AQP Gold winning team achieved the following results: improved safety 100%; reduced equipment downtime by 99%;

improved wood chip quality; developed skills in teamwork; and increased profitability by $54,000.[2]

Identifying Customers, Stakeholders and Other Outside Influences

It should be clear by now that in a culture of continuous improvement, the customer is king. Everything teams do is geared toward satisfying customer needs in the present, anticipating needs in the future and providing the best proactive service available anywhere. So one of the first questions a team must answer is "Who is the customer?" Obviously, a customer is one who purchases your product or utilizes your services. Ah, but that's only the beginning....

The first thing to keep in mind is that there is more than one group of customers.

I know that's not a great cosmic revelation, but what it means to the team is trying to juggle a number of customer needs and priorities at the same time.

Besides the customers, there is another group whose needs must be recognized and met. This group is called the stakeholders. Stakeholders are individuals or groups that have a vested interest in or have influence or impact on the purpose or process for which the team is responsible.

Other external considerations often include laws and regulations, societal trends and status of technology.

For example, when a healthcare company commissions a team to get drugs to the marketplace quicker, the team must immediately get to work identifying the key external influences that will affect its progress, e.g., requirements of physicians and hospitals, the FDA or drug retail chains.

Priorities and Focus

Just as Rome could not be built in a day, neither can an effective, improvement-oriented business culture. During their initial sessions, teams are likely to come up with a list of goals. And someone has to prioritize them.

In ad hoc continuous improvement teams and most newly formed teams, it is the responsibility of management or an experienced team leader to set the priorities and maintain the team's focus on these priorities. The manager or team leader is usually guided in determining priorities by the team's vision and mission and considering information about needs, issues and problems. Steering committees and key sponsors within the organization can also help guide teams in the priority designation process.

To identify the "vital few" problems, many teams themselves use such quality tools as the Pareto diagram (please see chapter 7, "Tools and Techniques").

Continuous improvement teams may use other criteria in the selection of process improvement projects. Uniroyal Chemical from Baton Rouge, Louisiana, a Gold Award winner in the AQP Competition sponsored by the Association of Quality and Participation, included factors such as safety, quality, productivity, environment and return on investment (ROI) as key criteria for improvement project selection.[3]

The Uniroyal team adopted a technique called "multivoting" that builds commitment to the team's choice through equal participation in the selection process. The multivoting steps include:
- Generate a list of problems through brainstorming.
- Eliminate duplicates and clarify meanings of team member statements.
- Record the final list of problems on a visible chart or board.
- Have each team member rank the problems in order of importance.
- Combine the ranking of all team members to arrive at priority issues.

One variation of this exercise has team members do all their ranking on a large board using little dot stickers to mark their choices. There are a million creative ways to conduct this exercise, as long as the end result is narrowing down large lists of problems or issues to smaller, more manageable lists of priorities.

Work and Improvement Process

It may seem as if I'm advocating spending an awful lot of time and effort getting all your ducks in a row in preparation for teaming. Well, you're right. And I guarantee you'll thank me later.

As I have already said a number of times, teaming requires a profound change in the mindsets and behaviors of organizations and individuals. To construct an improvement-oriented culture and work environment, we are asking people to change the way they systematically manage and continuously improve their work and processes. Being a team player isn't always as easy as it sounds, especially for those of us who were born and raised in a fiercely independent, entrepreneurial work world.

Once you've covered the basics of teaming, you are then ready to move on to the improvement process itself. This process has four distinct phases:

- Plan and Commit   Set goals, make commitments, establish measurement systems and develop plans for performing work.
- Perform   Carry out the plan.
- Check   Evaluate results.
- Act and React   Take necessary actions to bring results in line with goals.

Like a good breakfast in the morning, a good, well-thought-out beginning gives teams the nurturing they need to do their best. Without early definition and direction, major obstacles such as unclear goals or purpose often lead to ongoing conflict over roles and team tasks. As a result, the team will struggle and, eventually, may lose its momentum because of failure to take care of the basics in its early stages of development.

Summing Up

An important starting place for every team involves developing clarity about where the team is headed, what its purpose is, what it is trying to accomplish, and its principles and guidelines for behavior. One of the most formal methods of developing such clarity is by establishing a team charter.

This charter provides the team with a framework of operation, a place to begin and a clearly defined finish line. Without this important foundation, the team can quickly become unfocused, confused, lost.

During its initial (and later) planning stages, a team must always recognize and consider the needs of key customers and stakeholders. It must also identify other external influences, such as laws and regulations, societal trends and technological status, that are likely to have an effect on its work.

Workbook Section

Practice

TEAM LEADER

Prepare to develop a team *charter* that includes the *vision, mission* statement and *guiding principles*.

Prompt the team with questions such as: What are we hoping to become as a team? How can our team best use each individual's talents, skills, abilities and interests? What will our team be known for within our organization and by our customers? How will the products and services produced or improved by our team add value for our customers? Why are the work and the improvements we hope to make important to the organization and our customers?

TEAM MEMBERS

1. Develop your team's *vision*. To accomplish this, use the following steps:
    *   Each member is to develop a vision independently. Elements of that vision might be service or product quality, value to the organization or team climate.
    *   Form small groups to share individual visions. Some groups have found it helpful to use metaphors to help members develop and communicate a clear picture of how they see the team in the present and in the future. For example, in the beginning, members might envision the team as a thoroughbred colt, young and still a little wobbly on its feet, but destined for greatness. When looking toward the future, they see the team as a sleek, fast racehorse, capable of winning the Kentucky Derby. Or they may use automobile metaphors, imagining their team as the Cadillac of the organization.
    *   After each subgroup reviews its work before the entire team, identify common elements within the team.

2. Define a team *mission* that clearly and succinctly describes your purpose. Using the above information, create one clear

mission statement for your team. To accomplish this, remember to use the following steps:

- Each member should develop a team mission independently.
- Form subgroups to share individual missions, combine ideas and, using a visible chart, develop a joint mission statement.
- As a full team, review each subgroup's mission statement and underline key words that everyone can buy into. (Notice I said "buy into." The process may involve some deep discussion, perhaps a bit of arguing and some compromise—none of which are bad things, by the way—among team members.)

3. Develop your team's guiding *principles* using these basic procedures:

    - Brainstorm two lists, working first individually and then as a team.
       - List one: Identify the characteristics and practices of the best team you have been part of or have known about.
       - List two: Identify the characteristics of the worst team you have been part of or have known about.
    - Be specific when listing the characteristics, behaviors or practices. When thinking about characteristics, give thought to accomplishments and how it felt or could have felt to be associated with each of those teams.
    - Identify those items on both lists that pretty much everyone on your team thinks should be emulated or eliminated by your team.
       - Using the agreed-on items as a base, brainstorm a list of five to ten values (guiding principles) that will be most useful in helping your team establish itself as an operational unit.
       - Have all members discuss the pros and cons of each suggested guiding principle until the group arrives at consensus on a list all members can support. The

guidelines can be amended any time the team feels that a change is needed to keep the team operating effectively.

- When developing guidelines, be sure to keep in mind the following areas:
- Procedures for making assignments, rotating assignments
- Procedures for cross-training
- Procedures for holding short, effective meetings
- The types of decisions to be made by consensus and decision-making roles
- Procedures for resolving conflicts and airing disagreements

TEAM LEADER

Facilitate a team discussion to develop priority goals for the group's direction.

Develop some success measures to track your team's progress toward these goals.

Sample goal: Reduce cycle time by 20 percent

Measures: Non-value-added steps identified by the first quarter; improvement plan designed and implemented by May 30. Follow up inspections and cycle time measures completed by July 8.

Identify obstacles that can get in the way of achieving your goals. Brainstorm actions and contingencies that can be included in your plans to ensure success reaching your goals. Chart these obstacles and actions/contingencies. Then determine who in the team will be responsible for handling the obstacles and initiating the actions/contingencies. Add that information to the chart. Finally, determine a timeline for the responsible parties and add that to the chart. A sample chart might look like the following:

OBSTACLES	ACTIONS/ CONTINGENCIES (WHO? WHEN?)	RESPONSIBILITY
Operations people may resist new system changes Quality Control people may resist new sampling scheme	Conduct an orientation session Develop a step-by-step guide Have a formal training session on sampling Establish a hotline for inquiries	T. Hanks 5/5 B. Strand 7/30 W. Hill 8/4 W. Billings 9/11

Key Tips

If you are just beginning the launch of a team, don't try to save time by skipping over the development of a team *charter.*

Remember, a charter is not set in cement. It should be a flexible document to be revisited periodically by the team for appropriateness.

If your team is responsible for an improvement initiative (either continuous improvement or reengineering) be sure to clearly identify the boundaries (starting and ending points) of the process you are improving.

It is also helpful to seek clarity about the expectations of key "influencers" whose commitment you will need in order to develop viable solutions. Key influencers may include sponsors of the team, important leaders within the company, and other external and internal people known to be able to influence change in your company.

3

LEADERSHIP
AND TEAM ROLES

The team efforts at a unit of a large financial subsidiary in New Jersey produced an increase in customer satisfaction of more than one-third and a fourfold increase in profits in less than a five-year period.

If you have ever been a member of a team, you may have personal experience regarding what can happen (and not happen) when the team is stuck with an ineffective leader. If there is anything more frustrating and demotivating, it is trying to work on a team where there is role ambiguity or confusion. That can get positively ugly.

We know that the success of a team is closely related to its leadership and the interactions between leader and members, and among the members themselves. Everyone on the team must have a role. And the role of the leader is to serve as a guide, an advisor and a continuous source of support. To put it in its simplest terms, the role of the leader is to lead.

Some elements of leadership, referred to as "organizational leadership," must come from people outside the team. Organizational leadership can come from management, from team sponsors within the organization, from steering committees, etc. It usually takes the form of broad direction and alignment, help and support, encouragement and reinforcement, or resources allocation or authority.

Other elements of leadership are associated with task accomplishment and group interaction. This leadership may come from an experienced team leader right from the beginning. But it is not unusual for it to have to come from outside the team (i.e., from a manager or sponsor) in the early stages of the team's development. However, as the team matures, the members need to continuously transfer leadership responsibilities to the team itself. It is expected that, in time, the responsibilities initially assigned to a designated team leader will be assumed by the team as a group.

This shift in leadership is more apparent—and necessary—in teams that are organized around the self-directed or self-managed approach. However, it can also be extremely beneficial for process improvement, reengineering and ad hoc cross-functional teams. In these cases, the team leader can gradually empower members to make decisions, delegate responsibility for action, and move toward more of a coaching role (versus command role) during a transition from one-person leadership to shared leadership. This process can make a big difference in how quickly and effectively teams can move toward building commitment and ease into high performance mode.

The Dual Focus

One of the things that makes the team leader's task such a challenging one is that it constantly requires the leader to focus on two key functions at one time. One is the management of tasks to which the team is assigned. It is the leader's job to ensure that the work gets done and accurate decisions are made. The other is management of group interaction, ensuring that members interact in ways that are appropriate and productive in the course of carrying out the team's responsibilities.

In traditional organizations, supervisors were expected to consistently provide task and group interaction leadership. They decided how the work would be done, assigned individual responsibilities and managed all processes. Since there was little involvement on the part of the rest of the work group, this work structure was usually characterized by a low level of commitment on the part of its members.

As I explained before, in the new team culture, the team leader may still need to provide this form of leadership in the early stages of a team's development. But as the team matures and grows in its capabilities, the leadership must come from the team. If it doesn't, the commitment necessary for team progress and success may never develop.

The most successful team leaders I've witnessed in my external facilitator role are those who give their teams a jump-start in the early stages. By that, I mean they start out by providing their teams with all the necessary structure and detail they need to get started. However, being the farsighted leaders that they are, they pay less attention to tasks and more to goals at this stage in the team's development. They also put a great deal of emphasis on group dynamics and relationships. In other words, they make sure the group members move toward becoming a team.

Some of my most recent research on leadership competencies indicates that a set of what I call "social interaction competencies" will be required of leaders in the next century. These social inter-action competencies include coaching, fostering open communication, empowering others, inspiring enthusiasm and influencing others. These skills will become increasingly important as companies come to rely more and more on their teams for high levels of performance and achievement.

Task leadership can vary with the type and nature of the team. However, it usually includes these responsibilities:

- Ensure that correct and effective methods are in place for problem-solving, decision-making, planning and defining role and responsibility.
- Facilitate to evaluate the team's performance and assignments.
- Conduct meetings to facilitate progress toward goals.

Group interaction leadership (relationship leadership) focuses on how team members work together to accomplish results. Responsibilities in this area include the following:

- Ensure effective interaction and participation.
- Facilitate conflict management.
- Ensure that unproductive behavior among team members is modified and guiding principles are used.
- Promote a climate of openness, honesty and trust.

The Shift

Significant development may need to occur among team members before they are ready, willing and able to take over the bulk of the responsibilities of leadership. This shift is less dramatic in teams that are in existence only for short-term continuous improvement efforts than in teams focused on longer range projects or when operating in more permanent cross-functional or self-directed formats. No matter how modest or how dramatic the transition, it is usually a challenging process—for both the team's members and its leaders.

This is particularly true for team members and designated team leaders who have previously worked in the more traditional work settings where leaders were highly structured in their roles as commanders and disciplinarians. Initially, leaders might be uneasy about relinquishing total control. Team members, used to having a know-it-all boss to turn to (and blame) may be seriously bewildered by the realization that no one has all the answers. And they may be uncomfortable taking on the burden of responsibility for their actions and results instead of being able to toss their problems over the wall to let someone else handle.

Team leaders must be able to make the shift from dictator to facilitator in their minds as well as with their actions. They must develop the skills to coach, inspire, motivate and communicate and, perhaps most difficult of all, become comfortable with relying on the expertise of others.

Team members must develop their confidence as well as their skills. They must develop the skills to work without a safety net, so to speak, and to advance with caution, but without fear.

Roles and Responsibilities

To prepare members for their team-based leadership, each individual must be assured that he or she plays an important, valuable and valued role in the team's activities. Success is the ultimate confidence-builder. So when team members see their ideas and efforts succeed, their motivation to do more will usually grow.

Whether the team is a continuous improvement team, a reengineering team or a natural work team of a self-managed or cross-functional nature, roles and responsibilities must be carefully designated, understood, and carried out with dedication and commitment.

Typical responsibilities that can be delegated to temporary improvement teams include:
- Preparing meeting agendas
- Leading meetings
- Completing assignments
- Collecting data and gathering information
- Publishing meeting minutes
- Critiquing meetings
- Making presentations
- Writing proposals
- Implementing planned improvements

Roles and responsibilities delegated to members of teams that are designed for long-term activity may include:
- Work planning and scheduling
- Troubleshooting
- Ordering supplies
- Performing minor maintenance
- Record-keeping
- Training
- Performing other designated tasks or activities

Initially, it is up to the leader to ensure that roles, responsibilities and accountability are clearly defined and understood. Later on, as team members get to know each other, roles and responsibilities can be shifted to capitalize on the strengths and capabilities of each member.

Teams are much more likely to be successful if roles and responsibilities are designated to reflect member interests, capabilities and personal styles as much as possible. Members can also use their individual skills and expertise to cross-train one another. This cross-training allows for the sharing and rotating of assignments and responsibilities so team members can experience maximum variety and flexibility. Because members who are cross-trained can better understand and help one another, this exercise can also build stronger, more effective teams.

Management Control	Employee Involvement and Empowerment →					Employee Commitment and Self Management
Supervisor decides and informs or "sells" employees on the decision	Supervisor presents ideas and invites questions	Supervisor presents decisions subject to change	Supervisor identifies needs and problems, asks for input, recommendations	Supervisor identifies needs and boundaries and turns it over to employees to improve	Team leader defines requirements and monitors results	Team leader defines requirements and constraints, provides authority and removes obstacles
Employees implement and "get even"	Employees implement and complain	Employees implement and try to change	Employees participate in problem solving and process improvement to a limited extent	Employees participate in process improvements and problem solving, but work roles and responsibilities remain unchanged	Team selects and organizes its own work and reports results	Team is responsible for work inputs and outputs, quality, productivity, costs, improvements and measuring results

Figure 3-1. Continuum of Employee Involvement and Empowerment

Figure 3-1 depicts a continuum of employee involvement and empowerment. It also shows how the roles and responsibilities shift and grow for both the work group and the supervisor or leader as employees become more empowered and, therefore, better able to work as an effective team.

Supervisor's Role	Responsibility	Team Leader's Role
Translate, communicate and implement goals	Goals	Provide information, require measurements and goals, communicate direction and focus
Plan and schedule resource application and implementation	Planning	Provide information and support planning and scheduling by the team
Request and allocate resources	Resources	Provide authority to request and allocate resources; assist in obtaining resources
Coordinate application of resources (right time, right quantity, etc.)	Coordinate	Interface and coordinate with the team's external suppliers and providers
Control application of resources to meet plans and schedules	Control	Prioritize so that the team can control resources to meet plans and schedules
Measure and monitor implementation, progress and results	Measure and Monitor	Require self-measurement and monitoring; periodically review progress vs. goals and measurements

Figure 3-2. Traditional Supervisor vs. Team Leader Roles.

Reading Figure 3-2 from left to right will allow you to follow the shift in supervisor roles as the team matures. Currently, there are very few organizations operating at the three lower levels depicted in the figure. Most are operating somewhere at the three levels shown at the upper right of the figure. The shift in roles at the upper three levels is dramatic and requires a significant shift in culture, training and leadership style.

Self-Managed Teams

Probably the team approach that offers the most dramatic contrast to the traditional working culture is the self-managed or self-directed team. Unlike many other teams, the self-managed team is created for long-term functioning. Though self-managed, the team still needs team leaders.

The transition to self-managed team requires a major shift in culture, training and leadership style for everyone involved. The following is a look at how responsibilities are designated in this revolutionary organizational structure.

Team Member Responsibilities

Team member responsibilities in a self-managing work system typically include the following:

Problem-solving. Solutions must be found to problems that are likely to prevent the team from meeting commitments, achieving goals, attaining performance levels or satisfying customer requirements. Organizations that excel in this area typically provide extensive training to teams in problem-solving tools and techniques including Pareto charts, cause and effect analysis, brainstorming, scatter diagrams, stratification, and design of experiments. Some of the most effective teams I have ever encountered or heard about (including the Texas Instruments "Silicon Trek: The New Generation" that won an Association for Quality and Participation Award)[1] use a variety of these problem-solving techniques to identify root causes of their process problems.

Planning and scheduling. To help team members plan and schedule work and improvement activities effectively, superior companies provide everything from basic training in planning to advanced project management sessions.

Customer service. This involves being sensitive to customer requirements, measuring service levels and initiating improvements to maximize customer service and satisfaction. Top-notch groups may even learn how to develop and implement customer satisfaction surveys or at least get some consulting support in this area.

Cost and budget control. Manage costs and monitor budgets.

Measuring and reporting. Measure performance levels, results and accomplishments. Monitor processes. This is an area in which teams often seem to need help. Frequently, teams resist measuring because they are used to relying on gut instinct. Some fear that formal measuring methodologies may be overused in the evaluation of their work. In other instances, measuring may be a less than welcome task because it takes additional time for the team. Measuring and reporting can also be important to continuous improvement or reengineering teams since they need to establish a baseline measurement if they are going to accurately determine how successful they are with new improvement solutions.

Production and delivery of products and services. Perform the necessary work and provide the products and services expected from the team.

Quality: Ensure that quality standards are met and that products and services conform to requirements. This may involve significant communication among team members early in the new workflow process.

Managing and improving processes to meet customer requirements. Provide input and make recommendations and decisions on issues directly impacting work areas, processes and customers. Even though self-managed teams start off with newly designed processes, the most successful companies promote a continuous improvement mentality among teams (often referred to as "renewal") since customer requirements will change with time.

Team member selection and orientation. Ensure that each new member has the necessary experience, skills and attitudes to be effective and to provide the orientation necessary for rapid assimilation. In many cases, this is a new responsibility for team members; it should be a focus of team development efforts, particularly in firms that have traditionally left this to supervisors or managers.

Training and development. Each member takes responsibility for cross-training other team members and offering special assistance to those who may be less skilled to enhance their performance. Members use their own expertise to raise the competence level of the entire team. This can be a monumental effort for members of a self-managed team since, as members of such a team, they have usually already been assigned additional responsibilities and challenges. To handle the additional responsibility of cross-training takes time and good planning so that it will not interfere with overall team productivity.

Safety and environmental management. Ensure that safety and environmental practices are being followed and standards are being met. These responsibilities are absolutely critical at manufacturing sites. This responsibility may be rotated among team members in a self-managed environment.

Facilitating team interaction and meetings. Use appropriate group facilitation skills to ensure team interaction. In my experience, self-managed teams meet often, particularly in their early stages of development. The ability of each team member to be proficient at meeting management often has an impact on how effectively they work and how successful they are in providing products and services to the business unit.

Team Leader Roles

Although a team leader may play a hands-on role at the outset, the goal is for leaders to move toward a hands-off role as the team evolves and becomes truly self-managed. During this evolution, the leader has a number of day-to-day responsibilities and duties. The following are some of the responsibilities and behaviors that characterize this leadership role:

Organizational leader. The team leader provides vision, purpose, strategy, priorities and direction for teams consistent with those of the organization as a whole.

Successful team leaders with whom I have worked have typically prepared a kick-off meeting during which a significant amount of information and discussion is shared with the members. The leaders then schedule regular meetings to review key information and keep the team abreast of changing priorities. Effective team leaders are good at providing ongoing communication, providing direction and keeping the team focused on that direction.

Coach and mentor. Develop the team and create a supportive environment. Ensure that all necessary training and learning takes place. This includes training from appropriate outside sources as well as cross-functional training and support among the team members themselves. One team leader I know was an excellent coach and mentor for a self-management team. She made sure that the team was provided with all the training it needed, not just at the beginning, but also "just in time" when specific tools or techniques were needed by team members. She also made sure to meet team members' individual needs, spending time with them one-on-one as more focused coaching was needed.

Information resource. Provide feedback and information regarding changes from external and internal forces that may affect the work of the team. This feedback constantly offers the team a real-world perspective, thereby having a significant impact on the team's decision-making, planning and problem-solving activities. These information gathering and sharing responsibilities require the team leader to meet on a regular basis with the organization's top leadership and key stakeholders to monitor shifting expectations, participate in benchmarking visits so the team can compare their work to best-in-class practices, and stay informed of customer satisfaction and requirement data to ensure that the team stays focused on external needs.

Facilitator. Intervene when necessary to ensure that the team is making decisions, addressing issues, resolving conflicts, reaching agreements appropriately and working effectively. The best team leaders I've seen are well-trained in group facilitation techniques and can usually drive teams toward consensus. They are also able to spot conflict and intervene before a conflict gets out of hand.

Team liaison. Ensure effective interface with other teams. One financial services unit I consulted with had the motto "shared skills and shared success." Team leaders in the organization were good at sharing information with other teams and learning from other team leaders' experiences. They understood that teams could save a lot of time and energy by learning from one another what has worked—and what hasn't worked—and by sharing information about activities, successes and setbacks. These leaders were also able to run interference for their own teams and to work to remove real or perceived barriers to progress.

Resource provider. Provide the team with the resources necessary to meet commitments. Early in a team's life, these resources may be training and coaching. Later the team leader may need to secure time, managerial support or systems support for additional process improvements. A team of high achievers looks to the leader to give them the resources to get the job done and remove obstacles.

Process consultant. In addition to guiding the team through the process of examining the external environment and modifying work systems to respond to customer needs, the leader also keeps track of the team itself as it progresses and matures. The top leaders I have known have been able to occasionally stand back from the actual work processes and review the status of the group as a team. Some leaders actually use written surveys and have the team review the consolidated results for clues about what the team might need to become more productive. In some companies, team leaders have a budget for hiring external consultants to help facilitate such team evaluation. However, the reality is that many companies don't have the financial resources to use an outside person for this task. In these cases, the responsibility for this important function is assigned to the team leader.

Advisor. Help the team meet its objectives by advising on goal setting, problem-solving or other administrative functions assumed by the team.

Role model. Model the behaviors, processes and principles that the teams are expected to adopt. In other words, you have to "walk the talk." Teams are quick to pick up on team leaders who don't practice what they preach.

A poor model can lead to further conflict within the team and lack of commitment among its members.

Reinforcer. Catching people doing things right is a practice that is crucial for motivating individuals. The same goes for teams. That's why one of the most important roles the team leader can play is as reinforcer, the one who gives recognition, acknowledgment, the "attaboys and girls" when earned by team members for positive behaviors and accomplishments, development and maturity, teamwork, changes and responses, and approaches and creativity.

Summing Up

From the outset, team members and leaders must have a clear idea of their roles and responsibilities. All teams, even self-managing ones, have a great need for strong, competent, effective leadership.

While the shift over time toward empowerment of the team as it develops and matures is inevitable, the team leader's ability to let go and the team members' abilities to assume new duties are imperative as the transition progresses.

As you consider longer term team structures, such as self-managed teams, think carefully about these responsibilities and the leadership shift necessary for success, particularly if you have influence in the selection of leaders or members of teams.

Workbook Section

Practice

TEAM LEADER

Lead a discussion of the elements of task and group interaction leadership with the team. Ask:

If task leadership is not coming primarily from within the team, what elements are lacking? How can the team obtain these missing elements?

To what extent is the group interaction leadership coming from the team? To what extent is it coming from the team leader?

If group interaction leadership is not coming primarily from within the team, what elements are lacking? How does the lack of those elements affect performance? How can the team obtain the missing elements?

Review your roles as leader with the team. Have them identify those that you are performing today. Have them identify roles they would like to see more or less of, and those they would like to perform themselves.

TEAM MEMBER

1. Review your team roles. Identify those roles your team is performing today. Identify those that you want to do more of. Discuss those roles with your leader.

2. Complete the Team Member Leadership Assessment.

Team Member Leadership Assessment

Using the following scale, assess the overall level of task and group interaction leadership demonstrated by team members:

1 = Not demonstrated by any team members
2 = Demonstrated by some team members occasionally
3 = Demonstrated by some team members some of the time
4 = Demonstrated by most team members some of the time
5 = Demonstrated by most team members most of the time

Task Leadership   RATING
Team is using correct and effective procedures   _____
Responsibilities are defined and understood   _____
Planning and coordination of team activities   _____
Assignments are made and completed   _____
Goals are established, performance is monitored   _____
The necessary decisions are being made   _____

Group Interaction Leadership   RATING
All members are involved and contributing   _____
There is effective interaction between members   _____
Conflicts are resolved effectively   _____
Decisions are being made by the team when
    appropriate and by individuals when appropriate   _____
There is a climate of openness, honesty and trust   _____
Agreement is reached appropriately   _____
Unproductive behavior is modified   _____
The team is working together effectively   _____

For items rated 1 or 2: Discuss with your leader and create a plan for developing team leadership practices.

For items rated 3 or 4: Discuss within your team and create a plan for further developing leadership practices.

3. Complete the Work Team Responsibilities Assessment.

Work Team Responsibilities Assessment

Using the following scale, assess the handling of work team responsibilities demonstrated by team members:

1 = Not a team responsibility

2 = Not a team responsibility, but plans exist and development is taking place for the team to assume this responsibility

3 = The team has assumed this responsibility recently and is enhancing its capability to perform more effectively

4 = The team is responsible for this item, but not all members are fully qualified to perform

5 = The team is responsible for this item and all members are qualified or close to being qualified to perform this task reasonably competently

ASSESSMENT	RATING
Responsibility	_____
Problem-solving	_____
Training and development	_____
Planning and scheduling	_____
Customer service	_____
Quality	_____
Cost and budget control	_____
Production and delivery of products or services	_____
Measuring and reporting	_____
Team member selection and orientation	_____
Identifying customer requirements	_____
Managing and improving processes to meet customer requirements	_____
Safety and environmental management	_____
Facilitating team interactions and meetings	_____

For items rated 1: Discuss with your team leader and determine what the timetable and plan are for preparing the team to take over this responsibility.

For items rated 2 to 4: Are you and your leader satisfied with the progress? If not, why not, and what steps can be taken to improve?

Key Tips

If you are just getting started with teams, consider the key responsibilities for team leaders and members before selecting candidates. Some organizations moving to team-based designs actually require candidates to write letters explaining why they want to be part of the team.

Make sure you provide sufficient training to team members and team leaders to prepare them to assume new leadership responsibilities.

Periodic evaluation of the team, by the team itself, is warranted throughout its life. Although the formal team leader may facilitate this initially, teams typically move toward peer evaluation as the team matures. Initially, members may resist the concept of peer evaluation (after all, it can, at first glance, seem a lot like being a tattletale at school). But as the team matures, members should become more comfortable with this exercise and even find it a positive learning experience.

If your team gets stuck when it comes to clarifying responsibilities, use a role and responsibility matrix. This can be used when a team is being organized to clarify general responsibilities or with specific projects to assign key tasks to individual members or subgroups of a team.

Action Items	Team Member Responsibilities			
	MEMBER 1	MEMBER 2	MEMBER 3	MEMBER 4
1.				X
2.			X	
3.	X	X		
4.	X			
5.			X	

To be successful, a supervisor from a traditional environment transitioning as a leader to a team-based environment may need ongoing feedback and support from both inside and outside the team.

4

THE TEAM'S DOMAIN

Domain: a territory in which dominion is exercised.
— *Webster's Ninth Collegiate Dictionary*

Federal Express promises to deliver a package by 10:30 A.M. the next day and to be able to pinpoint the location of any package at any time. This level of performance comes at some cost to the customer as well as to the company. If neither speed of delivery nor traceability are particularly important to the sender or recipient, then these are not critical attributes for the customer. Therefore, the company would probably gain little by promoting the valiant efforts by employees to live up to this next day delivery guarantee. However, Federal Express has determined that its primary customer base does consider speed of delivery and traceability as crucial, so the company has designated them as key values that are constantly repeated and reinforced at the management level and at every other level throughout the organization.

In the global economy, quality and service are defined by the customer. The organization that is unable to determine what is important to the customer, unable to deliver what is important to the customer, or unwilling to make changes to accommodate customer needs and preferences, is one that is destined for a rude awakening in the very near future. In fact, for many companies, that awakening has already come. Unfortunately, for some it came too late.

The words "quality" and "service" refer to the degree to which a business—and each of the components that make up that business—is ready, willing and able to deliver on promises that match their customers' needs and expectations. A business may deliver on its promises to a high degree, but if these promises are not important to the customer, then the company is not providing quality or service as the customer views it. In other words, that business has a big problem. Good intentions and hard work are only the first steps toward quality and service. Without identification of and responsiveness to real customer needs, the company simply cannot deliver the quality and service today's customer demands.

A quality organization is one that knows its customers' requirements, has made promises related to those requirements, and delivers on those premises. The ability of an organization to deliver on these promises requires:

- Working backwards and translating customer requirements so the company can produce targeted products and services and use internal processes capable of meeting those requirements.
- Ensuring that all people and processes are committed to those requirements, and are capable of delivering flawlessly on internal and external promises.

Quality-conscious companies make sure they monitor customer requirements and conduct surveys to ensure that their business processes are capable of meeting and perhaps even exceeding critical customer requirements. On the other hand, companies that haven't quite caught on to the quality concept don't do a great job in either monitoring customer expectations or making adjustments in their business processes to meet changing customer needs and expectations.

Team Boundaries

A true customer-focused team knows the boundaries of its domain, as well as what must take place within those boundaries to provide high standards of quality and service. This includes knowing all the parts of the workflow that might have any impact on what the team produces for its customers and what it is necessary for managing and improving all of those workflow elements.

Some organizations have redesigned themselves so that one team of people has responsibility for an entire process, starting with the inputs from the external suppliers to delivery of the finished product or service to the external customers. In this situation, the team domain is easily definable. For example, let's say a team has responsibility for an order fulfillment process. In this case, the team would identify and track all of the key workflow actions that relate to completing an order for its customers. The team would identify all its key suppliers (e.g. sales representatives in the field), its sources of input (e.g. the customer order form), the team's own internal processes (e.g. the picking and packaging of the order) and the outputs (e.g. a finished on-time delivery) it provides to its customers, which could include an internal unit that the team hands-off to (e.g. shipping) or the ultimate external customer (e.g. retail store, distributor or consumer).

In many organizations, however, this whole project approach to teams is not feasible because of the complexity of the work or the nature of the workflow. Under these conditions, the organization might consist of a series of teams. In this structure, each team would be responsible and accountable for major segments of a process. Each team also would be linked to all the others, with one being the supplier to the next and/or being the customer of the previous team. Figure 4-1 depicts the flow of work across the organization, moving from one team to another in an internal supplier/customer relationship. Figure 4-2 identifies the elements of a team's domain.

In the situation where teams are linked in an internal supplier/customer relationship, it is even more important for each team to be clear on its boundaries and the conditions of hand-off or transition. If each team is not clear and comfortable with its parameters, a great deal of time and money could be wasted, conflict generated and errors made.

For teams that do not have direct interface with the external customers, it is absolutely imperative to ensure that they communi-

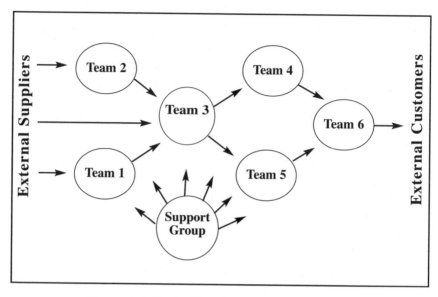

Figure 4-1. Work Flow Across the Organization

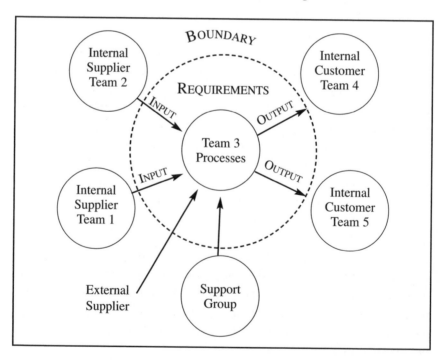

Figure 4-2. Elements of a Team's Domain

cate and respond to the needs of their internal customers (i.e., other teams). This is the only way to ensure that the voice of the external customer is heard by every team and properly translated to them.

In summary, the most effective teams I meet in quality organizations have a clear view of their internal and external customer requirements, and they work hard at adding value to the products and services they produce for both. Only if each team is effective can the organization as a whole provide the competitive products and services external customers seek.

Methods

Analyzing and Defining Team Domain

A team defines its domain by addressing the following issues and questions:

CUSTOMERS

Who are the external customers that directly receive products or services from the team?

Who are the internal customers (departments, other teams, etc.) that receive products or services directly from the team?

What other internal requirements are important to consider?

CUSTOMER REQUIREMENTS

Prioritize and identify the most critical requirements for each major customer group based on your current knowledge. Define customer requirements in specific and measurable terms. Consider such characteristics as quality (be specific), accuracy, speed or cycle time, timeliness, availability, flexibility or adaptability, functionality, cost, performance, reliability, durability, serviceability and accessibility.

VALIDATING CUSTOMER REQUIREMENTS

Meet with major customers to obtain input on specific needs and requirements. Often organizations do surveys or receive ongoing evaluations from customers or a sample of customers to stay current with customer requirements.

Analyze the information obtained from customers. How does the results compare to your original knowledge?

Identify the most significant requirements. Many teams, after collecting data in subgroups, will outline their findings on easel paper and make it visible to all the team members. The entire team will analyze all the subgroups' data for themes and implications for their work.

Process Requirements

Identify the major processes for which the team is responsible. Typically, I find the best way to do this is to identify how your team's process fits into the business unit's core process. Get a conceptual view of your workflow by breaking it down into five to seven steps. Then develop a more detailed view so that delays, rework, and other forms of waste can be identified.

Make sure you also identify external and internal suppliers to the process.

Identify major inputs (materials, financial responses, information, services, products, advice, etc.) and their sources.

Establish quality requirements for significant inputs. You know what they say—GARBAGE IN, GARBAGE OUT.

Communicate quality requirements to suppliers and establish a measurement and feedback system. Many times the companies with the highest quality also have superior supplier and partner programs.

Validate Your Process

It's not a bad idea to get customers, suppliers and other work partners to validate the process description that your team has developed. One process improvement team I worked with displayed a large map of their process in the cafeteria of their headquarters. This gave everyone from the company the opportunity of providing, through the use of various colored post-it notes, input on delays, rework, defects and other errors they observed in the team's process. This technique provided an enormous amount of information for the team to draw upon while developing improvement solutions.

Team Performance Measurements

Based on customer data, establish measurements for the most significant requirements.

Implement measures for your internal processes, particularly those that will affect outputs to your customers.

Establish score cards for major customer groups as a tool for measurable feedback. Remember, what gets measured gets improved!

CONTINUALLY IMPROVE

Even if you have a new team and new workflow process:

Identify and solve problems as they arise.

Reduce or eliminate activity that customers would not see as valuable.

Identify and reduce variation.

Work with suppliers to improve inputs and reduce variation in workflow.

Redesign the process if you need higher levels of performance. Some of my clients have found that their older processes are too broken and filled with non-value-added activity to fix. They just start from scratch and redesign new processes that are better suited to satisfying current and future customer requirements.

APPROACHING THE CUSTOMER

It is important that your team approach your customers with an open mind and in a nonthreatening, nondefensive manner. Customers need to understand that the team is merely seeking information and reactions and is prepared to listen and respond to them. It is best for the team to prepare the approach in advance, so that the interaction will be worthwhile and will help to improve relationships.

You can approach a customer in two ways:

A face-to-face *interview* enables you to use prepared questions to start and to ask follow-up questions, based on the customer's responses, in order to get more specific or detailed information. It is recommended that an interview be used for the initial data-gathering.

A *questionnaire* enables you to gather information without taking as much of your time. Use questionnaires after initial interviews to keep your information up-to-date.

The following guidelines can help you prepare for and conduct the interview:

Ask open-ended questions to determine the importance,

desired levels and current satisfaction levels of the customer for the services/products you deliver.

Ask your customers to identify any other significant requirements that you may provide to increase his degree of satisfaction.

Ask follow-up questions when you are given a vague or general response.

Ask customers if they have noticed any changes, over a period of time, for better or worse, in the products or services you provide for them.

Ask customers to suggest improvements in your products or services that might help the team to better meet their requirements.

Ask internal customers to explain how their requirements relate to the requirements of external customers.

Ask customers about changes in their business that might have an impact on their requirements in the future.

Provide customers with an opportunity to ask questions or bring up particular matters of importance to them.

Avoid being defensive or attempting to explain why you do things the way you do, or why your products or services are the way they are.

Encourage customers to express their feelings.

Summing Up

Discovering your team domain can help add focus to your team's purpose and give you an extended view of all the parts of the workflow that produces the products or services your customers need and want.

By keeping an eye on the customer you get a fix on the most important person in the work equation. By reviewing all of your workflow steps and measuring their effectiveness, you can avoid costly errors and be well on your way to continuous improvement.

Workbook Exercise

Practice

TEAM LEADER

Facilitate a discussion of major external/internal customers. Have the team set priorities for key customers from that group.

Identify in specific, measurable terms major external and internal customer requirements.

Lead a discussion of views from the team to determine how it is meeting requirements. Any opportunities for some quick solutions? Are there problems that need further analysis?

TEAM MEMBERS (WITH CONSULTATION FROM YOUR TEAM LEADER OR CONSULTANT)

Develop an interview guide to obtain specific information from your customers with regard to requirements, satisfaction and performance. Then use it to interview customers.

Analyze the customer interviews. Use this information to develop team performance measurements and, if data suggests the need, a performance improvement plan. Based on the results, establish improvement goals.

Key Tips

Make sure when identifying your team domain that you begin by looking externally at the key customers and their requirements. Too often teams get tunnel vision by focusing on their own internal workflows. Only by examining your customers' responses are you going to be able to identify what's value added (i.e. something the customer would consider important), and therefore worth including in your workflow.

Make sure you validate customer requirements and process steps. Too often we think we know about our customers and workflows. My experience, however, is that by validating their information most teams gain additional insights about requirements from their customers and additional insights about problems in the team's processes.

Don't forget to measure. In many corporate cultures, measurement is not usually reinforced or rewarded. As a result, more often than not, any attempts at introducing measuring methodologies within the culture are initially resisted. It is only through measurement that we can obtain baselines which the team can improve. By measuring, we can prove our worth as a team to our business unit!

5

TEAM MEETINGS

Have you ever attended a meeting and come out wondering why you did? Did the meeting seem unnecessary? Did the leader lose control or neglect to follow an agenda? Perhaps you just thought the meeting was a complete waste of your time! Well, you're not alone. For many companies, meetings should be one of the first things targeted for improvement.

Among the most common complaints I hear are:

"The meeting wasn't needed!"

"They never start on time."

"They go off on tangents."

"The right people are never there."

I could probably fill the rest of these pages with more of these complaints but my guess is that you have already heard them, or expressed them yourself.

What's surprising is that when you consider the time people spend in meetings, particularly in team-based cultures, there is probably a lot of wasted time and unproductive effort in U.S. companies! Bottom line: Waste translates into a lot of lost dollars.

In many companies it can be difficult to speak personally with a leader because so much of the leader's time is tied up conducting and attending meetings. But without effective meeting leadership and participation, the communication necessary for quick and accurate decision-making can be blocked.

So we have to recognize meetings as a necessary fact of corporate life. Let's face it, few people have all the information and knowledge necessary to make intelligent decisions on complex matters. And meetings become even more essential as employees become involved in day-to-day management.

However, the other side of the coin is that if the teams doing the work are spending too much time in meetings, the work will not get done, and performance and customer satisfaction will suffer. The good news is that if meetings are truly effective, work is getting done!

Meeting Basics

Be sure to identify a specific purpose and good reason for people to attend a meeting. Although that may sound like pure common sense to you, just think about how many times you've attended meetings only to ask yourself, "Why am I here?" If the meeting has no purpose, it should not be called. Or if a particular person's input is not needed, that individual should not be asked to attend.

Meetings can serve a variety of important purposes. They can be useful for helping team members:
- Share information and learn from each other
- Review team performance and/or discuss improvement strategies
- Set goals, develop plans, and organize responsibilities, activities or assignments
- Solve problems or work on process improvements
- Make decisions.

Before calling a meeting, think about whether there might be a better way to communicate or accomplish the goals of the meeting through informal methods such as working lunches with one or two colleagues, memos, phone calls, e-mail, etc. If there are more effective ways, try to use them first. Too often I hear of meetings conducted on items that could have easily been handled with a simple conversation on the plant floor or office corridor. In today's hi-tech world, there should be many methods pursued before considering a meeting that will tie up lots of people's time and company resources.

In many companies team meetings are held on a regular basis and several goals are pursued. In reality, however, a shorter meeting held to accomplish one specific purpose can often be more effective than a longer meeting held to accomplish multiple purposes.

Team meetings typically take place:

- *Daily* to discuss operational matters. Daily meetings are usually short in duration (fifteen minutes or less) and are held to discuss the previous day's events, upcoming events for the day, problems or conditions experienced by a previous shift (typically in manufacturing), daily work activities, schedules and assignments.

- *Weekly* for longer-range planning; deciding on rotational assignments, roles and responsibilities; information sharing; reviewing performance data; discussing problems; and, perhaps, discussing progress on an ongoing problem-solving activity.

- *Biweekly or monthly* to review performance data such as costs and budgets, customer feedback and quality, and to develop action plans for improvement.

- *Ad hoc* (when needed) for solving an operational problem.

- *Weekly or biweekly* for keeping up with workflow issues.

Meeting Preparation

In order for meetings to be effective and to help the participants accomplish their goals in the shortest amount of time, important details need to be considered before, during and after the meeting. When I am presenting information on meeting management to teams, I often show a video starring John Cleese (of *A Fish Called Wanda* fame, the British comedian from Monty Python) called *Meetings, Bloody Meetings*. In the video it is emphasized that before a meeting, it is important that a meeting agenda be written and that you notify team members and other necessary participants in advance.

Everyone should receive a copy of the agenda in advance of the meeting, so they can come prepared. It is the responsibility of the meeting leader or a designated member to do the planning and set the agenda based on input from the other members. Figures 5-1 and 5-2 can be used as a notice for an ad hoc or multipurpose meeting. Figure 5-3 can be used for a weekly team planner and notice.

Meetings must have structure, methods and procedures. Effective group interaction is needed to ensure participation and ownership.

I'm sure you have attended some effective meetings recently. What was it that you observed that made those meetings successful? The most successful meetings I have seen involved three elements: designing and sticking to an agenda, using good meeting facilitation techniques to elicit team discussions for each item, and taking actions to ensure that team members carry out assigned tasks.

Having an agenda prepared and distributed is a critical step in meeting planning. But even the most well-planned agenda is meaningless unless it is followed at the meeting. Of course, there will be times when a genuine crisis or critical issue not included on the agenda needs to take precedence. That's understandable, even expected. But it should be the exception, not the norm.

In fact, smart team leaders will have the team establish meeting norms (or ground rules) for meetings early in the launch of the team. These norms can be very helpful in preventing the team from going off track from the agenda.

For an ad hoc or multipurpose meeting, the agenda should be designed so follow-up actions—or completion of tasks assigned at previous meetings—are discussed first. A discussion of new items, beginning with most important and ending with least importance, should follow. This way, if time runs out, the priority items will have been covered. (Figure 5-3 provides a model for sequencing and recording key items of a weekly team meeting.) Savvy meeting leaders also put time allotments alongside agenda items so that appropriate discussion time is allocated to key items.

Meeting Notice

Where and When:_____

Purpose: _____

_____

_____

Goal(s): _____

_____

_____

Participants: _____

_____

_____

Preparation Required: _____

_____

_____

_____

Agenda Items: _____

_____

_____

_____

_____

General Comments: _____

_____

_____

_____

_____

_____

Figure 5-1. Meeting Notice

Meeting Planner/Notice

Team:

Where & When:

Purpose:

Start and End Time:

Other Participants

FYI:

Description of Agenda Item	Person Responsible	Desired Outcome	Approx. Time	Preparation Needed

Miscellaneous:

Figure 5-2. Meeting Planner/Notice

Weekly Team Meeting Planner/Recorder

Team _____ Date _____

I. INTRODUCTION, AGENDA REVIEW

Agenda Items: _____

_____

_____

Action Item Review / Status Report: _____

_____

_____

II. NEWS AND INFORMATION

_____

_____

_____

_____

_____

III. TEAM PERFORMANCE REVIEW (SELECTED MEASUREMENTS)

Performance Area   Results/Status/Change

_____

_____

_____

_____

_____

IV. RECOGNITION OF TEAM MEMBERS

Who   Why   How

_____

_____

_____

_____

Figure 5-3. Weekly Team Meeting Planner/Recorder

Weekly Team Meeting Planner/Recorder (page2)

V. Problem Solving/ Process Improvement/Issue Resolution
Item and Status: _____
_____
_____

Discussed: _____
_____
_____
_____
_____
_____

VI. Team Member Issues and Concerns
Item and Status: _____
_____
_____
_____
_____

VII. Summary and Assignments

Action Item	Who	Due Date

VIII. Miscellaneous
Next Meeting Agenda Items: _____
_____
_____
_____
_____

Agenda Format

The suggested sequence for a weekly team meeting is as follows:
- Welcome, introductions (non-members, experts, customers in attendance) and agenda review.
- Action item review: Status reports on action items from previous meetings.
- Communicate news and information from within and outside the team.
- Review team or department performance.
- Recognition of team members.
- Discussion of team work issues.
- Discussion of team members' concerns.
- Summary of the meeting's key points and action items.
- Issues for the next meeting.

Discussion Sequence

The second priority for effective meetings is using a logical sequence for discussing each item before moving on to the next item on the agenda. Follow this sequence:
- Explain the goal of the discussion.
- Gather information related to the issue.
- Discuss alternative actions for accomplishing the goal.
- Assign responsibility.
- Summarize and move on to the next item of the agenda.

Meeting Facilitation

Effective meeting leaders must have well-developed meeting facilitation skills. It is no exaggeration to say that these skills can often make the difference between a poor meeting leader and a good or excellent one.

One of these facilitation skills deals with ensuring that all meeting members have the same understanding of issues and actions. For example:

After observing perplexed expressions on some team members' faces, the leader might say: "Let me be sure I am clear on this. Are we saying that the customer wants a new design?" In this instance, the leader is helping the team clearly define the issue at hand.

It is also the leader's responsibility to move the discussion forward when there is a delay or confusion (which I often refer to as the team getting stuck in the mud).

For example, the leader might say: "Let me suggest that we put that aside for now and come back to it when we discuss design changes. Do we have agreement on that?" These little interventions by the meeting leader will be required at times if the meeting is to stay on track and on time.

Other critical facilitating behaviors for meeting leaders include the ability to:

- Acknowledge, respect and praise others' contributions
- Seek ideas and input on solutions
- Resolve conflicts by bringing out all relevant information
- Encourage diversity and differences
- Check for agreement among members.

Meeting Ground Rules or Norms

As I mentioned earlier, norms (also referred to as codes of conduct) can be helpful to the team leader and members by establishing the ground rules of conduct for all the team's meetings. Some basic norms include:

- Meeting will start and end on time.
- No interruptions.

Ensuring effective participation requires its own set of rules such as:

- Listening intently.
- It's okay to ask questions.

As more technology enters the meeting scene, I see other ground rules developing. Some examples are:

- No beepers.
- Silence your pagers.

Of course, I have had the opportunity to facilitate some wild and crazy groups. Here are a couple of real-life ground rules you probably haven't come across before (and probably won't need for your own meetings—the situations that required these rules provided some interesting challenges!):
- No biting.
- No attacking.
- No throwing of objects.

Meeting Follow-Up

If the team is to accomplish its objectives, three things need to take place at the end of one meeting and before the beginning of the next:

Evaluate the Meeting

Members should be asked their opinions and asked to provide specific feedback to the leader. To get the process going, the leader might ask:
- How effective was the team from a task standpoint (such as sticking to the agenda, use of time, use of appropriate problem-solving techniques)?
- How effective was the group interaction?

The evaluation may be a structured discussion or a form that can be completed and discussed. It is healthy to recognize the good points of the meeting, but most of the discussion should focus on items needing improvement. (Figure 5-4 provides an example of a meeting evaluation form.) Members' evaluations should include suggestions for improvements.

Document Results

Second, the results of the meeting should be put into writing and distributed to team members, to others participating in the meeting, and to those interested in or impacted by the outcome of the meeting. (Figure 5-5 is an example of how to summarize the results of a meeting and provide a preliminary agenda for next meeting.)

Team Meeting Evaluation

PRACTICE	RATING
Agendas are prepared and distributed in advance.	_____
Team members prepare for their participation in meetings.	_____
Meetings start and end on time.	_____
Each meeting has a clearly defined purpose and expected outcome.	_____
Our team has established ground rules and follows them for meetings.	_____
Our team sticks to the agenda in meetings	_____
Participation is good and evenly balanced.	_____
Team members listen attentively.	_____
Diversity of opinions is encouraged.	_____
Conflicts are resolved objectively and diplomatically.	_____
Task facilitation practices such as checking for understanding are used	_____
Group facilitation practices such as asking questions, seeking and acknowledging ideas are used.	_____
Meetings end with summaries and reviews of assignments.	_____
Team members follow up on assignments.	_____
Meetings are evaluated and improvements are undertaken.	_____

Assess the overall level of team meeting effectiveness demonstrated by team members using the following scale:
1 = never; 2 = occasionally; 3 = sometimes; 4 = often; 5 = always

Comments: _____
_____
_____
_____
_____

Figure 5-4. Team Meeting Evaluation

Meeting Summary

Team _____ Date _____

In Attendance: _____

_____

_____

_____

SUMMARY

Discussed: (Agenda items, conclusions, decisions)_____

_____

_____

_____

_____

_____

_____

ACTION ITEMS

Action Item	Who	Due Date

NEXT MEETING

Preliminary Agenda: _____

_____

_____

_____

Figure 5-5. Meeting Summary

Carry Out Assignments

Third, team members must complete the actions agreed to and assignments made or the team will fall short of its goals. Often when team members aren't committed to following through on their assignments, they only delay the team's initiatives since many of the members are relying on completion of all key actions by all of their teammates. Failure by one or a few members can delay improvement initiatives or other projects several months particularly if project plans have been set in motion and a member's lack of action interferes with the critical activities needed to get the improvement project done on time and in a quality manner.

Summing Up

Meetings can be exciting, stimulating and productive. They can also be a complete waste of time.

Great meetings require preparation from both team leaders and members.

If you are leading a meeting, make sure you've developed and communicated an agenda. Make sure you follow it.

You may need to consider some training in meeting facilitation skills. It can make a big difference for you and your team.

Whether you are a team leader or member, always remember the meeting norms established by your team. These norms will help the entire team stay on track.

I can't overemphasize the need for documentation and completion of meeting assignments. After all, the whole point of any meeting is not just to talk about getting things done; it's to make sure they actually get done.

Workbook Section

Practice

TEAM LEADER

Develop an agenda for your team meeting. Use the following checklist for agenda appropriateness:

___ Agenda is prepared and distributed in advance.

___ Agenda has defined a purpose and an expected outcome of the meeting.

___ You have prepared for participation by assigning items to team members when appropriate.

___ You have allocated specific time spans for major agenda items.

___ You have allotted time at the end for a summary and evaluation of the meeting.

Conduct a brief evaluation of your next meeting. On a piece of easel paper, note with a marker a + (plus) sign on one side of the paper; on the other side note a Δ (change) sign as illustrated:

+	Δ

Solicit feedback from the group to determine what went well. Note these comments on the plus (+) side. Then ask the group what needs to be done differently at the next team meeting. Note these comments on the change (Δ) side.

Thank the members for their feedback.

TEAM MEMBERS

Before your next meeting, review this Top Ten list of suggested meeting guidelines for team members:

• Complete individual assignments before the meeting.
• Start on time.
• Abide by meeting ground rules.
• Stick to the agenda.
• Listen attentively.
• Encourage diverse opinions.

- Participate.
- Clarify by asking questions.
- Acknowledge ideas.
- Share your experiences.

Key Tips

Being prepared for meetings will help your team make them effective.

As the leader, don't take sides in meetings. Make sure all points are heard. In moving a group toward agreement, make visible points of agreement and disagreement.

Don't assume you have consensus just because team members don't say anything about a particular suggested course of action. Have a discussion and make sure all members agree to live up to and support a decision on items your team has decided require consensus. Some teams use signs to indicate agreement such as "thumbs up."

Don't forget to summarize at the end of a meeting. Often, no activity takes place between meetings because the meeting leader failed at the conclusion of the meeting to summarize action items and ensure follow-up by team members.

It helps to capture ideas visibly during the meeting. A chart posted with the title "Parking Lot" is often used to collect ideas that may not necessarily be part of the current meeting agenda, but may warrant revisiting by the team at a later time. A posted chart entitled "Action Items" can help capture follow-up actions that may surface during the meeting. The team can then review this list to ensure that all necessary actions are assigned and follow-up occurs after the meeting.

If you are leading the meeting, make it easy on yourself. Assign roles such as timekeeper or scribe. Why place the burden entirely on yourself? These meeting roles also help get others involved.

6

STAYING ON TARGET

One team standardized some of its plant site's processes, reducing paperwork 66 percent and product development time from twenty-eight weeks to nine weeks.

According to my trusty source, *Webster's Ninth New Collegiate Dictionary,* a goal is "the end toward which effort is directed: aim." It is a desired future state or outcome that typically reflects improvement from the current state.

Goals, like measurements, can help your team focus its efforts on improving areas that are important to customers and the organization. Goals play an important role in helping a group of individuals come together as a team with a shared sense of purpose. Without common goals, such a group can never hope to become a team.

Five Steps for Setting Goals

From the beginning, your team needs to translate its general direction and priorities into specific, measurable goals that support your organization's higher-level goals. The following five steps outline the process for setting meaningful goals:

Determine your team's domain. Identify those areas that are your team's responsibility and that will be examined in evaluations of your team's performance.

Identify your team's priorities as dictated by your department or organization's broader goals. One pharmaceutical organization which has been a long-term client of mine makes it a standard practice for teams to complete a form outlining all external and internal requirements and assigning priorities based on the organization's broader goals. This way the team can compare internal and external requirements and set priorities accordingly, using such criteria as quality, cost, change impact, financial impact, delivery, and work environment impact.

Review current performance measurements and determine whether they are meaningful and appropriate.

Establish SANE goals for your team. SANE is the acronym for specific, attainable, numerical (so they can be measured), and energizing. These goals will help clarify the leader's, and members' expectations of the team.

To monitor your team's progress, use your team's success or failure to attain these SANE goals. Evaluate the team's results in terms of impact on the attainment of the organization's goals.

Why Measure?

Granted, measuring results takes extra time, work and, sometimes aggravation. So why bother to do it? The answer is that measurement provides information on how well your team is managing its areas of responsibility. It also provides a basis for recognizing the team, the individual members and their successes.

Measurement not only identifies problems but also helps to spotlight the process areas that need improvement. And, measurement offers teams an opportunity to establish clear goals and attain them.

In the world of sports, measurement plays a significant role in determining a team's success. The most significant measurement is one team's score against the other's. Team statistics can also be a good indicator of how well the players are working as a team. Individual player statistics can reflect the individual's contribution to support the team's efforts. A coach also may use such measurements as the amount of time an individual practices to help identify areas of needed improvement and as a barometer for team success.

Many people are uncomfortable with performance reviews and measurements. Too often, people perceive measurement as something that is done *to* you rather than something that is helpful or is done *for* you.

There are many reasons why people are uneasy about measurement. In some cases, they have never had experience with measurement. And we all know that it's basic human instinct to be suspicious and uncomfortable with something new. For other people, the only experiences they have ever had with measurement have been negative. Instead of being used to recognize successes and point the way toward further improvement, measurement has often been used as a basis for criticism. Instead of putting the emphasis on what went right, the focus has been on what went wrong. No wonder so many people view measurement as a weapon wielded against them by management!

Early in my consulting career I visited a company that claimed to be customer-focused. After observing the customer service department for a period of time, I noticed a disturbing pattern. Many of the reps spent most of their time looking for someone to pass calls to and many who did speak to the customers stayed on the telephone for only brief periods of time with them. When I questioned the supervisor about these behaviors, I was told that they were being monitored for the number of calls they responded to. Obviously, problem-solving, resolution of customer issues or quality of the call didn't come into play in their measurement system.

Sometimes there can be too much focus on measured results and not enough focus on how those results were achieved. This can lead to short-term results but do nothing to ensure success in the future. For example, a team can focus so intently on meeting its immediate goals that it may sacrifice opportunities to make advances in the crucial areas of teamwork, individual and team development, team effectiveness, and interteam relationships. If this shortsighted trend continues, the team will not be able to build the internal foundation it needs for future advancement. Even worse, an exaggerated emphasis on short-term results can cause members to work at cross-purposes or feel pulled in opposite directions.

This is where an oversight committee such as a steering committee can be helpful, particularly during process improvement efforts. Such a group can review team goals, measurements and activities to ensure that everyone is pulling in the same direction.

In a truly customer-focused organization, there must be a balance between developing the internal effectiveness of the team and meeting the immediate needs of its internal as well as external customers. Only when that balance is achieved can the team effectively establish its goals, measurement indexes and improvement strategies. For example, a company trying to reduce inventory levels at the same time it is trying to fill orders faster and avoid back orders may, at first, seem to be pulled in opposite directions. However, this is just the kind of situation that can demonstrate the real value of teaming. In a case like this, an organization needs the perspective, creativity and problem-solving abilities of a team of individuals all working toward the same goals to come up with solutions that will support their long-term internal initiatives and, at the same time, satisfy customers.

This is why teams are particularly important when companies are updating their technology. Although management is concerned with immediate satisfaction of customer needs, it is also concerned with strategic goals that will enable them to maintain those customers into the next century.

Companies usually review their external customer requirements before looking internally. I think it is helpful to start with this external analysis to provide a basis for determining what outputs (goods and services) must be produced and what measurement methodologies should be used to monitor them.

After all, you have to understand what the customers want before you can meet their expectations. Let's say your company produces soft drinks. It only makes sense to ask what customers want or expect from that drink before you decide what gets measured internally to satisfy those requirements. I refer to this as the outside-in approach.

More on Meaningful Measurements

To ensure that the measurements your team selects are meaningful, there are several factors that must be considered:

Just as goals should be specific, so should measurements. They should focus on customer requirements, key workflow indicators that relate to those requirements, and support team and company goals.

Performance measurement should occur frequently and at set intervals. There should also be a mechanism for periodic feedback for the team. For example, let's say that I, like so many Americans, set a weight loss goal. In order to achieve that goal, I establish some key measures that I will monitor on a frequent basis. These measures may include the number of glasses of water I drink daily, and the amount of exercise I complete weekly. If I just develop those measures without monitoring them, I probably reduce my chances of achieving my weight loss goal. However, if I monitor these measures within a specific periodic time frame, I increase my chances of success.

Measurements should be adopted by the team. If members feel they have a stake in the results, they will support the measurement process. Teams have a tough time dealing with imposed measurements. When they are free to be creative and select critical measures that relate to their requirements, you may be surprised at the excellent outcomes and team commitment that are produced. In these situations, the team becomes involved not only in developing the measures, but in establishing implementation and follow-up plans as well.

Once I stopped a continuous improvement team at a quasi-governmental agency from implementing a pilot plan because they lacked any baseline measurements for their original workflow. Without these measurements, they had no basis for accurately monitoring their success. Instead of viewing my insistence on measurements with suspicion or annoyance, the team members were inspired by the challenge. It was gratifying to witness the excitement and creativity in the room as they brainstormed key methods to track their old process so they could ultimately measure the change that resulted from implementing their improvement solutions.

Tips for Selecting Meaningful Measurements

Use appropriate measurements for the team. Consider what makes sense based on your company's values and workflows. Notice, I said "appropriate measurements." There is nothing more revolting to people in a work environment than to have to monitor numerous measurements that have no significance. Make sure the ones you initiate are appropriate and tied to critical customer requirements.

Use measurements to change, improve and recognize the team. Remember to collect baseline data on your original workflow before you pilot or implement a change or improvement. It's the only way you will learn what impact your solutions have and how successful you are as a team. Measurements also provide an interim way to recognize team performance. You don't always have to wait until the ultimate goal is accomplished to reward progress.

Focus the team on how results are achieved, not just what results are achieved. This is where measurements using peer evaluation can come in handy.

Avoid measurements that put the team at cross-purposes or in opposite directions.

Types of Measurements

Earlier in this discussion, I alluded to a number of measurements that teams can find useful. Measurements can relate to the results of a team's work, or they can relate to the process itself. Most companies use one or a combination of the following:

Quality and service measurements gauge quality and service from the customer's point of view. They provide feedback on how well the products or services your team provides meet the requirements of their internal or external customers. Included may be measures related to meeting specifications, timeliness, durability, accuracy, and speed. Data for these measurements can usually be secured from customers through some form of customer survey and index. It is important to get information from customers that is as detailed as possible so the team knows exactly what to measure. I am particularly suspicious when I see measurements vaguely described as "on time" or "reduced." Exactly what is meant by "on time?" Does it mean within ten days...twenty...thirty? Exactly what is meant by "reduced?" Does it mean reduced to a twenty-day turnaround time or to less than ten complaints per month? Be specific.

One credit organization reported key customer data to employees on a regular basis. Every month or two, general sessions were held to allow the various work teams to secure updated information about how customers perceived the company based on their customer satisfaction index (CSI) measurements. It was a great way for teams to get feedback on their performance and maintain their focus on external customers.

Resource utilization measurements usually deal with costs, budgets, defects, rework, and waste. Many times teams look to the company's financial experts for assistance in developing sound resource utilization measurements. A number of top U.S. companies have taken up the challenge called Six Sigma, the reduction of defects to approximately three per million opportunities.

Process measurements evaluate the workflow of the process that produces the required quality and service results. They can also be used to evaluate the progression of team development. Process measurements typically fall into two categories: internal workflow measurements and input (supplier) measurements. If you are producing a soft drink, a typical customer may want a number of things from you as a manufacturer. These things could include a good tasting drink, a drink available at the store when needed, and a cheap price. In order to get those results, we could monitor a number of different measurements. Related internal workflow measurements might include a manufacturing process that produces a drink for less than 50 cents, a cycle time in producing the bottle at less than ten minutes, and a sample rated superior 99 percent of the time. Related input (supplier) measurements might include a specified quantity of water within eight hours from telephone call, or cost of raw ingredients not to exceed 35 cents per bottle. Obviously if the team is monitoring such process measurements, there is a greater likelihood that they will have better results—provided they have selected the right things to measure.

Team Measures

Each team should decide early in its history what measurements it should use to monitor and evaluate its own progress. For short-term improvement teams, such measurements may simply evaluate the team's progress against some agreed-upon project goal and timetable. The development of measurements for long-term self-directed teams may be a bit more complex and tied directly to the organization leadership's day-to-day business results and to performance expectations of the team. Team-based cultures in today's business climate are often measured on their overall contribution to the organization's total business results.

Forms of Measurement

What are the forms of measurement you should consider as a team? Here are some of the alternatives:

One of the most widely used forms of measurement is concrete value. These measurements include items such as the number of pounds produced, the number of tests performed, the number of complaints received and the time needed to complete any particular task.

Ratio measurements are another form and include such items as percent-on-time, percentage of rework, defects-per-million, and other ratios associated with productivity and waste in a team's workflow processes.

Ratings measurements include customer satisfaction, assessment of team effectiveness and assessment of the effectiveness of team meetings. Certain industries may tend to favor one specific measurement form over the others. For instance, in a recent visit with teams at National Broadcasting Company (NBC), it became quite apparent to me that ratings measurements are extremely important to their business since advertising revenue and other result areas are often based on ratings and viewer perception.

Methods

Once your team has determined what to measure and has started collecting performance data, the question becomes, "How do we evaluate the results in order to take action?" There are four reference points for evaluating performance. They include:

Past performance. If available, this data provides a reference for what has been done, and can indicate whether things are getting better or worse. Past performance data is more valuable for identifying the existence of a problem than for identifying opportunities for improvement or for providing motivation for future improvement. Even if no concrete past performance data exists, a current measure of performance can at least establish a baseline for future comparison once solutions are piloted or implemented. Make sure you take adequate samples of performance data so you have a valid reading of your processes. Don't take samples only early on Monday morning or late Friday afternoon. Past performance data is generally not considered by reengineering teams. They are more interested in what processes should be than in collecting historical information on what has been.

Customer requirements. These requirements are valuable indicators of whether your team's performance is acceptable or not, and to what degree that performance is exceeding your customers' requirements. If customer requirements are not being met, then obviously your team must take some action. Even when you are reviewing your workflow steps, you must continually assess whether the steps your team is using to process work are value added from the customer's perspective!

There are two important things I should caution you about, based on my experience with teams:

• In your eagerness to collect data regarding customer requirements, be careful not to inundate them with questions. You don't know what other groups within or outside of your organization may also be collecting data from these same customers.

It's not much of an exaggeration to say that answering survey questions could get to be a full-time job for customers, leaving little time for them to attend to their own businesses. So make sure the information-gathering methodology you choose (survey, focus group, etc.) is one that makes the best use of your customers' time. The goal is to choose a method that can help you glean the maximum amount of relevant information from your customers in the minimum amount of time.

• Don't expect yesterday's information to serve as a reliable guide to your customers' requirements today—or tomorrow. Some teams collect data once and assume that the information can stand the test of time. Unfortunately, customer expectations do change, and they're changing more rapidly now than ever before. You should develop careful plans for collecting new data at regular intervals to ensure that your information is current and your team's perspective is up to date.

Goals. These are your milestones along the road to improvement. They serve as a basis for planning and implementing one-step-at-a-time changes and taking corrective actions if necessary.

Benchmarks. Benchmarks provide a point of reference for your team to compare its performance and practices to the best-in-class performance and practices for a similar process or activity. When people think about benchmarking, Xerox is the most prominent company. This is the company that comes to mind because it installed benchmarking practices when it was losing its competitive edge to the Japanese. Benchmarking helped give Xerox the information it required to regain its prominent position in the marketplace.

You do not necessarily have to look to your own industry for benchmarks. I coordinated a visit many years ago for a team from a credit company that wanted to review and benchmark specific processes being used by a mortgage company. The credit company team applied its findings to improve some of the support processes within its own organization. When Polaroid was reengineering, it chose a customer fulfillment process as a critical core process. Instead of looking within its own industry for benchmarks, Polaroid decided to investigate L. L. Bean because of Bean's excellent reputation for customer fulfillment.

Four Sequenced Steps for Selecting Team Measurements

The following four steps can help your team determine what to measure and improve:

1. Determine your customers' requirements. Your team's products or services may have an impact on a number of internal and external customers. Therefore, you may need to set priorities as to what gets measured. Remember that some of your team's internal customers may also interact with your external customers. By sharing information with these internal customers, you may be able to glean a great deal of valuable insight into the requirements of your external customers. For example, the delivery and pick-up personnel from a van unit that calls on hospitals may be very helpful to the clinical lab representatives who are trying to learn more about the lab test needs of physicians and healthcare centers.

2. Determine what is important to the organization in terms of resource utilization and quality and service objectives. For example, if your team's objective is to deliver materials to a customer just in time to meet customer's requirements, delivery response time would be a meaningful measurement for quality and service. You also might want to set some measurements around inventory levels to focus on resource use.

3. Determine the key processes that need to be managed and improved upon. Make sure you establish monitoring systems and solicit team commitment to maintain these systems. Assign accountability for measurements within the team.

4. Determine what is necessary to improve teamwork and develop individual capabilities. This is particularly important if your team is going to be together for a long

time either in a self-managed or other type of cross-functional venture. Measurements will be important not only in looking at your workflow, but also in monitoring your performance as a team. Often, it's a good idea to identify the team's major goals during the early stages of its development and do some assessment of each team member so that individual development opportunities are identified based on the overall team's direction. Some teams I work with complete a training needs assessment or matrix that identifies all the areas of knowledge and skill development required by the team members to accomplish performance goals.

Summing Up

To stay on target as a team, you need to make sure that you have clear goals and team consensus on your targets. Make sure your goals are SANE and quantify them as much as possible. Don't forget to also designate times and dates for final goal completion and for interim actions along the way toward goal accomplishment. These steps will provide clarity and remove ambiguity for the team and those outside the team who might be evaluating its progress.

Measures are also critical to the improvement process. Results, resource utilization and process measures are the interim targets that will keep your team on the straight and narrow path to achieving its goals.

As I've mentioned before, don't forget to establish a measurement system for your team. It provides the team with a method of monitoring its progress and could help reduce conflict later.

Workbook Section

Practice

TEAM LEADER AND TEAM MEMBERS (JOINTLY)

Use the following categories to develop your team's measurement system. For each category the vital aspects of quality and service, resource utilization, process measurements, and team measures (behaviors, activities, etc.) can be determined by applying the six factors below:

What to measure

How to measure

Where to get information to use in the measurements

How to collect this information

Frequency of reporting needed for useful measurements

How the measurements should be presented

PROCESS MEASURES

Consider the critical workflow areas that can closely connect with your core products or services.

Consider the things you take in from suppliers to process as a team. Are there some critical measurements on which you can jointly agree for materials, information or products coming into your process? Remember: Garbage in, garbage out!

TEAM MEASUREMENTS

What are the critical member behaviors and activities that will have the strongest influence on the team's overall performance? For example: Perhaps the team concludes that the timeliness of completing assignments is an important measurement that should be an evaluation criterion for each member. Consider all the possibilities by brainstorming and then evaluate until you have developed a list of criteria that all team members can agree with and support.

Key Tips

Don't try to measure everything. You don't want to suffer from analysis paralysis. Just select measurements that make sense for the critical customer requirements you have identified and for important process and team issues.

When assigning values to goals and measurements, quantify wherever possible. The more quantifiable your measurements are, the less likely it is that they will be subject to a variety of interpretations.

Review measurements periodically. Original measurements may be less relevant in later stages of the team's development, and the team may decide at any point in time that other measurements are more critical.

Don't be afraid to share measurements with your customers or suppliers. In many cases, once suppliers understand your needs (remember you are one of their key customers), they will welcome the opportunity to help your team meet its goals.

7

TOOLS AND TECHNIQUES

No problem can stand the assault of sustained thinking.
—Voltaire

To achieve improvement, all of the following elements must all come together:

- A purpose or an objective
- The correct attitude toward improvement
- The right people working on the improvement
- A structured, systematic, disciplined approach to improvement
- Appropriate use of creative and rational decision-making techniques
- Use of facts and data, rather than opinions and suppositions
- Application of appropriate tools and techniques

Purpose and Sources of Improvement

How can a team know when there is a problem? Generally, the problem and/or need will be identified directly or indirectly by the team's customers, suppliers, process monitoring systems, or the team's own knowledge of what is and what should be. One summer I worked with a whole host of continuous improvement teams that were put together to improve critical processes within a quasi-governmental unit. The teams had been formed because the unit had received a ton of bad press about its workflows in a large metropolitan newspaper. In another situation, a continuous improvement team I facilitated was established after receiving some internal customer feedback from a facilities management survey that was periodically conducted among employees. The facilities management group wasn't happy with some of the ratings and comments and wanted to improve some support processes including intercompany mail.

Whenever a team takes on an improvement project, the reason should be well-defined and an objective should be clearly stated. Once an improvement situation is identified, the team should develop a specific problem or improvement statement (what and why?) and an improvement objective (how much or how far?). For example, one insurance company's improvement statement and an improvement objective was, "Reduce application entry processing errors by 30 percent, and the average time to process an application from the current twenty-five days to fifteen days, by the end of the year."

Attitude

Improvement requires a particular kind of philosophy or attitude. This attitude has four characteristics:
- It regards improvement as a challenge and an opportunity.
- It encourages everything, even problems, to come out into the open and is willing to take responsibility.
- It applies a disciplined and patient approach.
- It assumes that improvement is a never-ending process.

When methods and performance are being measured and the results are visibly displayed, it is human nature for a team to want to hide the fact that its performance level is not what it could be, or that a problem appears to exist. Your team should instead adopt an attitude that views the need for improvement as normal, and members should learn to regard any information that points out the need for improvement as helpful.

Your team needs to look for *what* is wrong, rather than *who* is wrong. Even if a problem is being created by a customer, supplier, another team or another part of the organization, your team should take responsibility for everything that goes on within its domain, and, along with that, the responsibility for improvement. Remember, no finger-pointing!

The hardest thing for anyone who has experienced a traumatic injury or who has just undergone difficult surgery is to get into a routine of disciplined rehabilitation. People who come back from "never-walk-again" injuries usually do so because they didn't wait for miracles or take shortcuts. Problems or improvements can be complex and difficult. Sometimes progress can be painfully slow. But in the end, the hard work, discipline and tenacity are worth it.

Teams must learn to view improvement as a never-ending process—as if it's a marathon or a race with no end. That doesn't mean there can't be a great deal of gratification and back-patting at designated points along the way. There should be time for celebration, but not for rest. Upon the achievement of every milestone, the team must take a moment or two to step back and admire their handiwork. Then they must view the same achievement again with a more critical eye and ask, "How can we make it even better?"

Although—or, more accurately, because—Wilson has long been a household name in the sporting goods business, the company is constantly looking for ways to improve their processes. A Wilson improvement team recently won a bronze award in the Association for Quality and Participation's team competition when, after a review of its golf ball manufacturing process, it improved the process by changing an outdated spindle-dependent manufacturing line. As a result, the company completely eliminated downtime, cut costs and reduced the number of defective golf balls it produced.[1]

Involve the Right People

Effective improvement requires the involvement of the right people. I don't mean people whose names are on some elite social register. In this case, the right people are:

- Members of the team who "touch" (or interact) with workflows within the team's domain
- Customers who benefit, or suppliers who need to adapt or improve
- Experts or support groups from the organization who can be helpful, or representatives from other teams who also have expertise.

Every situation may require the support of different resource groups. Therefore, before selecting the right people to assist your team, you must first consider your improvement or team goals. Resource people may be selected for their intimate knowledge of a particular customer's needs or a process targeted for improvement. Creative people are sometimes chosen to serve as devil's advocates for the team, to minimize the possibility of the group becoming complacent or developing tunnel vision.

Steps for Improvement

Step 1. Select

An ongoing team should keep a running list of improvement projects. In addition, that list should be reviewed on a regular basis and the priorities reset to ensure that critical needs are getting the attention they deserve. Customer needs should always be given the highest priority positions.

Step 2. Define

Define the problem and the desired improvement in specific terms. Then make sure all team members have a clear and similar understanding of what is expected. This sounds easier than it actually is. Teams often struggle harder than necessary to develop a clear and concise problem statement and/or improvement goal.

That is because the problem statement or the improvement goal they come up with isn't really a definition. It's a disguised solution. For example, "Reduce order entry processing errors by redesigning the form" is a disguised solution. A disguised solution severely limits the options that the team considers when identifying causes and exploring alternatives for eliminating those causes. A better definition of this same improvement project might be, "Reduce order entry processing errors by 35 percent." This clearly defines the problem and gives the team an improvement goal without suggesting that a solution has already been found.

Step 3. Analyze

Take time to analyze:
- Causes of problems
- Sources of variation
- Elements of waste and activities that customers wouldn't consider valuable
- Flow of process

Begin by brainstorming and listing all possible causes of problems and sources of variation or waste. Then select those that appear to have the greatest impact on process outputs and target them for improvement.

Step 4. Validate

Collect data to validate or verify the causes of problems or sources of variation in your workflows. Although, at first glance, this may seem to be a repetition of Step 3, the fact is that even though team members may be close to a process, it is possible that they don't know everything about it. Some of the information upon which the team has based its conclusions may be circumstantial. Sometimes additional information will be uncovered that does not support the results of the team's initial analysis. This step helps to guard the team against jumping to conclusions about the causes of a problem and fixing symptoms rather getting to the root and actually solving the problem. Without this validation step, the team may find itself constantly putting out fires that are bound to keep flaring up and diverting the team's attention and energies from working toward any real progress.

Step 5. Solve

Once the team has identified the causes, sources or factors of problems, and targeted the most important of these for improvement, it is time to develop alternative approaches or solutions for making the necessary changes.

Again, brainstorming should be your first step. This time the objective is to come up with a list of possible solutions or approaches. Then this list should be evaluated to select those solutions or approaches that appear to have the most potential for success.

If the cause of a problem is known, teams—particularly those involved in continuous improvement efforts—may be able to develop some "quick hit" solutions. For more complex problems, teams often need to use one or more techniques to find effective solutions.

Step 6. Implement and Monitor

In this step, your team will develop detailed implementation plans for the proposed improvement approaches or solutions. Some of the key elements that should be included in these plans are the "what, who, how and when." Your team must also set up a measurement process to evaluate the impact of the actions itemized in your plans. That way, you can accurately monitor if your actions are achieving the desired results or if you need to amend your plans or take additional steps.

Always remember that plans written on paper or discussed within the limited setting of the team may not work in the real world. You are probably already familiar with pilot projects used by major corporations to test new products or concepts on a limited basis, usually in a particular geographic area before attempting a full-scale roll-out. By piloting, companies can learn a great deal about how well a product or service meets customer needs, if any fine-tuning is needed or if, in fact, the product/service is unacceptable to customers before a great deal of time, money and energy is spent on introducing the product/service on a national or international scale.

This same piloting technique can also help teams test the viability and effectiveness of their improvement initiatives, whether they are major or minor. A new procedure for entering customer orders into a company's systems is a minor improvement; opening a new office in Atlanta with self-managed teams is a major reengineering project. In either case, teams can learn a lot from pilot projects and can implement necessary changes more effectively and successfully on a larger scale based on what they learn.

In the next section of this chapter, you will be presented with the techniques for carrying out the six steps just described. Some of the tools and techniques mentioned early in the section are particularly useful in the first four steps.

Techniques for Collecting Data and Information

Techniques for collecting data and information fall into two categories: recording data about events as they are occurring, and surveying people about their perceptions of events after they have happened. One way to record data about an event as it is occurring is to use checksheets. For example, to record how much time a customer service representative spends on the phone taking care of a customer, a checksheet might be used. To survey people about their perceptions of events, team members might use oral interviews or written questionnaires. An example of this would be interviewing customers to determine their priorities and to gauge how well the team is meeting their needs.

Beyond Checklists—The Questionnaire or Survey

A *checklist* is the most basic survey tool. It can tell you whether or not an individual or a team is performing a particular task appropriately or give you some indication of frequency relating to defects or problems with your workflow. There is little or no opportunity for in-depth discussion. At the other end of the spectrum is the *interview*, a face-to-face or at least voice-to-voice encounter that allows for explanation and clarification.

A questionnaire or survey creates a structured approach for obtaining the same type of information as an interview from a larger base of people in less time. While a questionnaire can be effective, this form of information gathering does have two distinct disadvantages. First, people may interpret the questions differently than intended by the preparer. Second, their answers may be ambiguous and there is no provision for asking follow-up questions based on responses.

Questionnaires are most useful when a large sample or database is needed. To pinpoint the issues and to refine and clarify the questions in order to garner the maximum amount of information from each one, the team should conduct a series of sample interviews with a select group of customers. It is often helpful for a team to conduct sample interviews among its own members to develop consensus before administering the questionnaires to customers on a larger scale.

Developing a questionnaire can take a significant amount of time. I have seen teams spend several hours—even days—trying to figure out the best way to phrase a question, whether open-ended or close-ended questions would yield the best information, what type of scale should be used and how long the interview should take.

Teams often engage professional help in questionnaire preparation by hiring a consultant or by seeking advice from interdepartmental staff. Market research departments will have valuable recommendations for developing effective questionnaires.

One of the first points to consider is how your team will conduct the survey. Will it be conducted through the mail, using focus groups, by telephone or by some other means? Will you consider some type of sampling—that is, do you need to interview large numbers of the targeted group or a small sample? Statistics can be helpful in projecting results. The team will probably need some guidance by its leader or a market specialist to determine the appropriate number of customers to survey.

Once the information is collected, your team needs to summarize, analyze, categorize and display the results. Many of the teams I have facilitated have focused more of their time on follow-up than they did in conducting the interviews. In many cases, this may be appropriate. After all, collecting the information is only the first part of your effort; it is how you analyze, summarize, learn from, and use the information that is most important.

Analysis Tools

Pareto Chart

A Pareto chart displays information so that the most significant or "vital few" causes of a problem or sources of variation are identified. It is a chart that lists the highest values to the left and the lowest values to the right; the values are listed in descending order from left to right. Perhaps you have seen them in such newspapers as *USA Today*. For an example, see below, Figure 7-1.

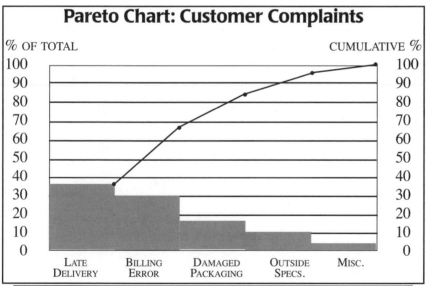

Category	Occurrences	%of Total	Cumulative %
Late delivery	38	38	
Billing error	31	69	
Damaged packaging	16	85	
Outside specifications	11	96	
Misc.	4	100	

Figure 7-1. Customer complaints plotted for analysis using a Pareto Chart

The 80-20 rule prevails in using Pareto charts: 80 percent of problems or opportunities stem from 20 percent of the listed items. Thus, the Pareto chart immediately directs attention to where the team effort should be concentrated to solve a problem or make an improvement.

Teams should use Pareto charts after conducting a survey or interview or following a review of performance data. The chart helps teams identify improvement opportunities and determine problems as well as causes of problems.

HOW TO USE A PARETO CHART

The accompanying illustrations (Figures 7-2 and 7-3) should help you to visualize how each step, as well as the final product, should look:

- Calculate and categorize the data collected; arrange the data in descending order in terms of value or frequency.
- Calculate the total and the percentage of the total for each category. If necessary, group the smallest categories into a single category labeled Miscellaneous.
- Draw a bar chart on graph paper with the left vertical axis representing the frequency, the horizontal axis representing the categories, and a right vertical axis representing the total cumulative percentage.

Checksheet – Customer Complaints
Summer, 1998

Type of Complaint	June	July	August	Sept.	Total
Shipping	5	7	5	8	25
Installation	5	5	5	5	20
Delivery	2	2	3	3	10
Service call	2	2	3	1	8
Telephone rudeness	0	0	1	0	1
Incorrect billing	0	1	0	0	1
	14	17	17	15	65

Figure 7-2. Checksheet for customer complaints

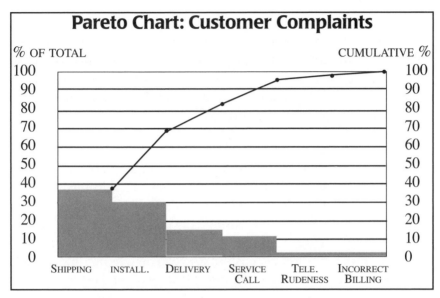

Figure 7-3. Pareto chart of customer complaints

- Working from left to right and in descending order, draw a bar for each category with the height representing the percentage of the total.
- Plot the cumulative percentage for each bar, moving from left to right, along the right axis.

In addition to helping teams target the vital few causes of problems, Pareto charts are an excellent visual aid for presenting project priorities, root cause analysis of problems and other key items analyzed by leadership, steering committees and others in the organization whose support might be necessary to the team's work.

Other Diagrams

The Scatter Diagram

Scatter diagrams show the relationship between two variables or changing conditions in a process. This method is frequently used during the analysis of data to determine the relationship of an element in a process to a defect or another element in the same process. For example, suppose after doing some analysis a team suspects that lack of training is a root cause of defects in a process. The team could do a scatter diagram plotting the number of hours of training against the number of defects to see if there is any type of relationship. This technique can be helpful in indicating or validating a cause and effect relationship.

How to Use a Scatter Diagram

Measurements are plotted as dots on a graph, with one variable on the vertical scale and the other variable on the horizontal scale. The resulting pattern will show if there is a positive, negative or nonexistent relationship between the variables.

The following Figure 7-4 shows a scatter diagram of customer order size versus customer age. The diagram indicates a positive correlation between customer order size and customer age. It is important to be cautious in your interpretation of these tools. Besides age, another variable such as income level may also influence the size of a customer's order.

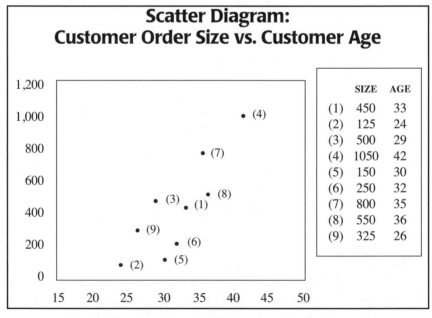

Figure 7-4. A scatter diagram of customer order size versus customer age

Cause-and-Effect Diagram

A cause-and-effect (C&E) diagram (see Figure 7-5), also referred to as a fishbone diagram because of its shape, provides a systematic way of looking at effects (or problems) and the causes (or sources) that create or contribute to those effects. Once completed, a C&E diagram will help your team understand the effects and the factors that influence them. It is one of the most common methods used among teams to find causes of problems.

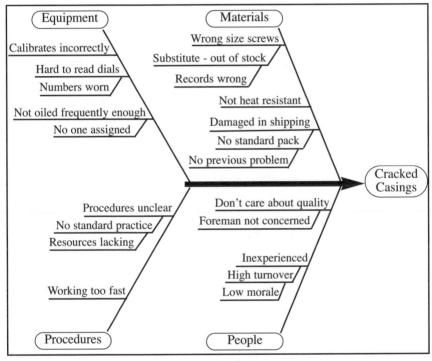

Figure 7-5. A sample cause-and-effect—or fish bone—diagram

Teams find the technique easy to use and helpful in narrowing down a problem to a vital few root causes. One team I worked with had a diagram that went around the four walls of a room. Obviously, they had quite a problem, with a number of potential causes. The team's biggest dilemma was trying to figure out how to narrow down the huge brainstormed list of causes to a vital few. Seldom do teams have to deal with a "fish" of such enormous size.

Typically a team can draw a comprehensive diagrammed analysis on one or two sheets of easel paper. There are also software programs that can be used to consolidate the information neatly for later presentations.

HOW TO USE CAUSE-AND-EFFECT DIAGRAMS

Decide on the effect or problem to be analyzed and write it in a box (or fish head) midway down and to the far right of a large sheet of paper.

- Establish four or five categories in which to organize the causes you will brainstorm as a team. In manufacturing environments, teams typically use people, machinery, materials, procedures and environment as categories. In other environments, categories such as methods and equipment may be added. The idea is to develop categories that make sense based on the problem (or effect) you have defined.

- Construct a diagram with each category representing a major bone connected to the center "backbone."

- Brainstorm possible causes or factors for each major bone. Draw and label these causes or factors as branches or small bones.

- For each branch, or small bone, seek underlying causes or factors by asking, "Why?" Continue asking "Why?" until there is no further answer. Usually asking "Why?" up to five times can help you identify the root causes—instead of just the symptoms—of the problem. Draw and label these underlying causes as subbranches.

After these first five tasks are completed, discuss and narrow down the possible causes or factors (sometimes a multi-voting technique may be used here). Attempt to arrive at a small number of likely causes. In Step 4 (validate) in the Steps to Improvement listed earlier in this chapter, you will collect data to substantiate or disprove that your suspected causes or factors are the most significant. You may even be able to use the scatter diagram to check the relationships between the possible causes and the effect under discussion.

Techniques for Creative Thinking

Brainstorming

Brainstorming is a process used to generate information by tapping into the knowledge of the team without the restriction or criticism that impedes creativity and free thinking. Teams often use this technique during data analysis and the development of cause-and-effect diagrams to uncover potential causes of a problem. This technique can be even more powerful a little later down the road when the team is trying to develop creative solutions to solve problems that have been identified.

HOW TO BRAINSTORM

You can't have a brainstorming session unless you bring the team together, whether physically or virtually, using technology. There must be active give-and-take between members so that ideas can be generated and built upon and information can be clarified. Once the team is together, members should:

- Define the topic and review the team's ground rules.
- Take a few minutes to allow each member to jot down his or her own thoughts and ideas.
- Share information by taking turns or by spontaneous contributions from all members.
- Refrain from questioning (other than to make sure the thought was properly understood or recorded), criticizing or ridiculing while information is being shared with other team members.
- Withhold judgments and evaluation until everyone has had a chance to speak.
- List all contributions and ideas on flip charts. (This job may go to the team leader, a designated facilitator or a scribe selected for the meeting.)
- Encourage "off-the-wall" ideas and "wild thinking."

Once your team has compiled a list of ideas, it is time to refine the information gleaned from the brainstorming. At this stage, the facilitator and team members have the opportunity to clarify, question or elaborate on any ideas for better understanding. In addition, if there are any similar ideas, they may be combined at this time. Except for duplicates, no other ideas should be eliminated at this point.

The next step is to organize the information so that it is easier to review. If the team is trying to find the cause of a problem, cause-and-effect diagrams can be helpful. Some criteria-based list reduction techniques (which will be reviewed later in this chapter) can help narrow down a list of solutions.

Mind Maps™

Mind Mapping is a technique originated by Tony Buzan that may be used to expand creativity by substituting free association for structured thinking. I have seen it successfully used in situations such as process reengineering to find innovative solutions. It also works well in teams made up of particularly creative people who may object to more traditional, rational, linear decision-making techniques. These creative groups usually find Mind Mapping to be a refreshing and inspiring change of pace.[2]

Mind Mapping can also be useful to predict what might go wrong in implementing an improvement plan or to identify any possible sources of resistance that might block the plan's progress.

HOW TO USE MIND MAPS

See Figure 7-6 on the facing page.

- Write or draw the problem, issue or situation that you are attempting to change at the center of a page.
- Identify and draw branches coming out of the central image representing the major categories. As new major categories are identified, draw additional main branches.
- As thoughts related to a branch are generated, draw smaller subbranches.
- As new associations are identified, continue to add smaller and smaller branches.

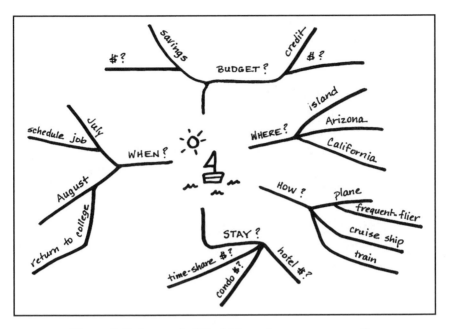

Figure 7-6. A sample Mind Map of a summer vacation

Although the whole point of Mind Mapping is to encourage structured free association, it is usually helpful to stay with a single main branch until ideas are exhausted. Just like brainstorming, team members should withhold clarifying, combining, sorting and evaluating until all information and ideas have been generated.

Once the Mind Mapping figure is completed and displayed, the team should narrow down the possibilities through discussion and other techniques.

Techniques for Objective Analysis

After using a creative thinking technique such as brainstorming or Mind Mapping, teams usually find themselves faced with a variety of options for fixing a problem, implementing a new improvement or solving other issues that have been uncovered during the discussion and analysis processes. That puts the team in quite a dilemma trying to determine which of these options is best, and which should be selected for implementation. In order to arrive at a decision everyone can be comfortable with, the team may want to consider using a technique based on objective analysis.

Criteria-Based Selection

This technique enables a team to objectively evaluate and compare a list of options against a predetermined set of criteria. It is used in steps 1 (select), 5 (solve), and 6 (monitor) of the Steps to Improvement described earlier in this chapter to arrive at the best approach and implementation plan.

HOW TO USE CRITERIA-BASED SELECTION

Brainstorm and develop a list of three to five criteria that are most relevant to the problem or desired improvement. Consider customer and organizational input including company goals, budget guidelines, etc.

- Weight each criterion. Ask which criteria are most important and rate them using a scale of 1–10 (10 being most valuable). Weight other criteria based on importance compared to your highest ranking criteria. Typical criteria might include least costly, fastest cycle time, minimum organizational impact, and timely implementation.
- Compare all options against the weighted criterion. For example, using "least costly" as the first criterion, start by considering which option is the least costly. Assign that your highest value, a 10. Then compare your other options and assign each a value based on how well it meets that criterion. Team members should rate each alternative individually before collectively coming to a consensual score.
- Multiply the criterion weight by the option score once you have compared all options to the criterion.
- Repeat this process for all key criteria.

Choose the best option across all the criteria. If you have two close-scoring options, you should also assess the risks associated with implementing each option.

EXAMPLE:

Criteria	Wt.	Option A Score	Wt x Sc.	Option B Score	Wt. x Sc.	Option C Score	Wt. x Sc.
Least costly	7	5	35	10	70	2	14
Fastest cycle time	10	10	100	7	70	9	90
Organizational impact	3	7	21	2	6	10	30
Timely implementation	5	10	50	3	15	8	40
Totals			206		161		174

In the above example options B and C have relatively close weighted scores. You may want to use one of the following selection techniques to select one option for implementation:

Multivoting

This technique provides a quick way to reduce a long list (ten items or more) of brainstormed ideas to a more manageable number.

How to Use Multivoting

- List all brainstormed ideas on a flip chart.
- Assign each team member a particular number of votes. The number of votes is equivalent to 20 to 30 percent of the number of items on the list—with a minimum of three and a maximum of eight votes. For example, for a list of twenty items, each member has four to six votes.
- Give each member one Post-It note for each vote, to be posted next to each item on the option list provided on the flip-chart. As an alternative, a show of hands for each item may be used.
- Repeat the process, if necessary, to narrow down the list to four options or fewer. Before repeating the process, remove items that received one vote or no votes. As an alternative, when the initial list is reduced to ten items or less, the criteria-based list reduction technique can be used.

- Team members should thoroughly discuss and evaluate each item on the short list. The team should then use a selection technique and consensus decision-making to select a final option.

Balance Sheet Selection

This simple technique involves dividing an easel or white-board into two sides, one side designated with a plus sign (+) , the other with a minus sign (-). For each option under discussion, team members should list the pros on the side marked with the plus and the cons on the side marked with the minus. Based on the results of this exercise, the group should be able to arrive at consensus on a choice.

Additional Tools and Techniques

A force-field analysis can help the team visualize the forces in a given situation that might help or hinder change and improvement. It can be particularly effective in step 5 (solve) to identify change needed for improvement, and in step 6 (monitor) to identify both the hindering and helping forces associated with implementing the proposed action plan.

A histogram is another useful chart to note variations in a given process. It presents a frequency distribution in bar form. When teams are analyzing (step 3) or monitoring (step 6) variations in their workflows, they often find this tool to be very helpful.

Run charts and control charts can also be useful for monitoring (step 6). Run charts can help pinpoint occurrences of a particular situation as well as identify trends, patterns or unusual situations for further analysis. They help observe and keep tabs on process variables and performance over time. Control charts are variations of run charts, using statistics to keep watch on common variations in a process and special events that might affect workflow.

Quality-focused organizations use these charts extensively and sometimes keep them posted so they can track how the important factors in their workflow are behaving day-to-day and know when a corrective action or additional analysis is necessary.

Many of the techniques I have described in this chapter as well as additional helpful hints can be found in a little book called *The Memory Jogger*™—*A Pocket Guide of Tools for Quality* published by GOAL/QPC.

I never leave home without it.

Summing Up

There is a six-step improvement process that teams should adopt when attacking any work issue. There is also a whole arsenal of tools and techniques available to help teams identify and solve problems and keep them on course toward improvement. Effective team members and team leaders take the time to become familiar with these techniques. They should also learn when and how each one can be put to best use to help the team achieve its goals.

Workbook Section

Practice

Team Leader

Have the team review the techniques listed. Discuss which might be applicable based on your current situation as a team. Identify which of these commonly used techniques your team members are unfamiliar or uncomfortable with.

Pick one or two techniques for review at your next meeting. Walk through the techniques using real-life examples based on the major work the team is now working on.

Have the team brainstorm a list of problems or projects to work on based on data that has recently been gathered.

Have the team prioritize and select an improvement project using the multi-voting or criteria-based selection technique.

Team Members

Brainstorm and use a cause-and-effect diagram to identify causes of a problem you have identified. Decide on a technique to select the vital few causes.

Design a data collection checksheet, interview, or questionnaire form and collect the data or information you need to validate the problem identified for further study in the previous step.

Brainstorm solutions or options for change. Use a technique to select the most appropriate solutions to implement.

Develop an implementation plan.

Key Tips

Remember there is more than one way to skin a cat. Many of these techniques can be useful at various stages or steps in a problem-solving or improvement process. The main idea is to use an appropriate technique that the team is comfortable with.

When brainstorming, don't get hung up on whether an idea should be posted. Just make sure you capture the idea and make it visible for the team. I have seen teams turn on a team member or team leader who used the power of the pen to filter ideas. Let the creative process occur initially without evaluation.

When you are doing problem-solving using the cause-and-effect diagram or another technique, make sure the team doesn't jump the gun and mistake "disguised solutions" for problem/improvement statements or improvement objectives. I have often observed teams develop solutions before they have decided on the root cause of a problem.

Remember to use the creativity tools. They can force people to think "outside the box" and develop some innovative solutions for your improvement efforts. Also remember that any extensive analysis you may develop as a team is worthless if it doesn't have the right impact on the company as a whole. So always keep your eye on the big picture as well as on your own corner of the world.

8

COMMUNICATION AND CONFLICT RESOLUTION

When two men in a business always agree,
one of them is unnecessary.

—Unknown

During my career, I have seen long-lasting, enthusiastic, high performance teams. I have also seen short-lived, unproductive, demoralized teams. The major difference between the two has been communication.

In these high performance teams, *members*:
- Freely and frequently share information with one another.
- Provide positive and constructive feedback on an ongoing basis.
- Work together effectively to solve problems and implement improvements without finger-pointing.
- Routinely interact with other teams, customers, suppliers, managers and resource providers.

Leaders of these teams:
- Reinforce their team's productive communication behaviors.
- Take time to actively listen.

- Provide feedback to the team as a group and to individuals on the team.
- Provide information that the team needs to do its job in an effective and timely manner.

The difference between the teams that practice these behaviors and those that don't can be amazing. In the first case, you have lively discussions, a high level of excitement and a universal sense of commitment. In the second case, you might wonder if you have walked into a room full of sleepwalkers. Members don't interact. They tend to look bored and uneasy. Like a classroom of children waiting for recess, they keep stealing glances at watches that never seem to move. If there are meetings, they are often more like lectures dominated by the team leader.

But don't be too dismayed if your team doesn't "click" immediately. Don't give up if the members are a little shy and maybe even nervous about speaking up. Communication skills can be learned. And, once these skills are learned, you might be surprised at how creative, innovative and productive your team can be.

Interaction Principles and Skills

Some people think communicating means talking...and talking...and talking. In reality, that's not communicating, it's filibustering. There are actually two sides to communication—the giving of information and the receiving of information. Both are equally important.

Getting people to talk is rarely a long-term problem. (In many cases, the problem may be getting them to stop.) The most common obstacle to communication, the one thing that most frequently prevents parties from connecting is poor listening.

When both parties are talking and neither is listening, that's one-way communication. Each is so intent on one viewpoint that neither cares nor is receptive to what the other is saying. We see this type of interaction when a referee and a coach are going at it in the field, screaming and hollering at one another. Each is focused solely on getting a point across. Instead of listening to what the other person is saying, each is too busy thinking about what to say next.

Two-way communication requires a combination of talking and listening. It requires each party to pay close attention to what the other is saying and to attempt to understand what they are hearing before responding. Good listeners are less inclined to make assumptions or to misunderstand what they hear.

There is also a third step to effective communication—the processing of the information given and received. People are not all the same. We have unique backgrounds, interests, capabilities and behavioral styles that combine to create highly individualized sets of perceptions, experiences, biases and emotions. These are the filters through which we process incoming and outgoing information. Unless your team happens to be made up entirely of kindred souls (which is highly unlikely), communication also requires a considerable amount of clarification and explanation.

You cannot force someone to communicate with you. If that person really chooses not to speak or listen, you can talk yourself blue in the face to no avail. But there are a number of techniques that can help you influence the process.

Nine Interpersonal Skills for Effective Interaction

Communication isn't just what you say...it's also how you say it. It takes strong interpersonal skills—nine of them, in fact—to initiate and maintain a productive and mutually satisfying dialogue. These nine crucial interpersonal skills (with examples) are:

Conveying means providing information or feelings, explaining, instructing, telling, informing or suggesting.

Tip: Plan what you want to convey. Address one issue at a time; be concrete, specific, and focused. I usually write down the major pieces of information I want to exchange before going into a team or one-on-one meeting. I find this particularly helpful when my goal is to influence the team or an individual. Advance planning enables me to be prepared to provide rationale and to sensitize people to my feelings on an issue.

Questioning is probing for more information, facts and details.

Tip No. 1: Use open-ended questions to encourage discussion and obtain as much information as possible. Example: "What are your thoughts on that issue?" or "How do you feel about that?" or "What happens as the order form enters your unit?"

Tip No. 2: Ask closed-end questions, which can be answered with a yes or no, to obtain a specific response. Example: "If I forget to verify the customer credit account, will the system still accept the order?"

Seeking is soliciting input, suggestions, ideas or involvement. Seeking typically takes the form of a question, but differs from questioning in that its purpose is to create involvement rather than obtain information. Seeking builds commitment and cooperation. The person who contributes to a solution will feel some ownership and will try hard to make it work. Example: "Can you give me some tips on how you would approach a situation such as this?"

Listening is paying attention, and translating what is heard into a frame of reference. Active listening is the most effective listening method. Some ways to actively listen include repeating what you heard, use of short interjections, summarizing and use of body language such as head nodding. Example: A good way to sum up a long meeting might be to say, "You agreed to do the following steps and I agreed to support you in these ways, is that correct?"

Rephrasing is assuring the speaker and yourself that you have not only heard but also accurately understood his or her message by rephrasing, or by repeating in your own words, what he or she has just said. Example: "What I think you are saying is that the team needs more funding to support this project."

Empathizing is showing the speaker that you recognize his or her feelings. When people communicate, the feelings expressed or implied are often as important or sometimes even more important than the words. Empathy does not imply sympathy or agreement. It merely implies understanding or recognition of a person's feelings, a basic necessity for effective communications and development of relationships. Example " I understand where you're coming from in this situation, let's discuss…"

Clarifying is asking for or providing additional information to improve understanding.

Tip: Do not ever assume that you are being clear or that you understand the other person. Ask additional questions and check for understanding. Example: "From the perplexed looks I am getting, it seems that I may have been unclear. What I meant to say is...."

Acknowledging is recognizing or complimenting someone for his or her contribution to the discussion. Acknowledging encourages greater participation. It does not necessarily imply agreement. Example: "I really appreciate your input. It has really brought us back on track to solve this problem."

Responding is replying when someone has conveyed information or feelings to you. Based on the nature of the conversation, your response may be agreement or disagreement, stating your position on the issue, presenting what you know about the situation or providing the information requested. If you agree, you may simply state your agreement and the reason why. If you disagree, state your position and reasons for disagreeing, then present your view without attacking the other person.

Interaction Process

Consider this process a planning strategy for interactions. It can provide a useful framework for applying the nine key communication techniques just discussed. You will be better able to organize your thoughts and determine how you will approach individual or team meetings.

To initiate involved discussion, follow this logical process:

Set the stage. Explain the subject, purpose and desired outcome of the conversation. Example: "I'd like to discuss the new product line and how we might make some design changes before the launch, so that it starts with fewer problems and higher efficiencies. Maybe we can come up with a proposal together."

Gather information. Ask questions, listen, rephrase and clarify, acknowledge, empathize and check for understanding.

Discuss. Initiate a dialogue.

Agree. Determine what actions should be taken and by whom. This usually occurs toward the end of the meeting so that everyone is clear about who does what following the meeting. Leaders who do this are more likely to achieve a greater degree of clarity at the end of meetings and greater productivity between meetings. Example: "Basically, you have agreed to follow up on the first two items we discussed today and I have agreed to check with Systems to see that you can receive the necessary resources to complete item three."

Close. End the discussion by acknowledging involvement and checking for understanding. Example: "I want to thank you for your participation today. Let me summarize the major issues we discussed and decisions we made…Does that make sense? Any questions?"

Conflict Resolution

Just as there are differences in people, so too are there differences in teams. You will rarely get unanimous agreement on most issues on the first try because team members have different opinions, experience levels, personal value systems, preferred ways of learning, styles of communication and personalities. There are also fundamental differences in team chemistry, the way members interact and the way the team operates as a unit. One team may prefer heavy analysis. Another may work best when the members are having fun. With individuals or teams, there's only one thing you can depend on—there will be differences. So you had better learn to deal with them if you hope to turn your team into an effective working unit.

Differences in people can be a source of creativity and lead to unique approaches to problems and improvements.

Differences are a problem only if there are no reasonable means to resolve conflicts. When that happens, people dig in their heels and relationships can be damaged. Conflict resolution allows the team's differences not just to coexist but also to benefit the team and its function.

Conflict Resolution Strategies

There are four basic strategies for resolving conflicts. Three of them don't work. It shouldn't be hard to pick out the one that does:

Avoidance. Both parties pretend a problem doesn't exist, hope it will resolve itself, or try to live with it.

Competition. One or both parties attempt to meet their own needs without concern for the other.

Compromise. Both parties agree to a resolution that, at best, partially meets their individual needs, but may result in a solution that doesn't make either one of them happy.

Mutual problem-solving. Both parties work to develop mutually satisfying solutions that meet all of their needs. To do this, each party must be assertive about his or her own views, then be able to listen to, understand and consider the other person's point of view. The end result should be consensus and mutual support.

Conflict Resolution Principles

The following principles will enhance your team's ability to resolve conflicts:

Explain the problem in detail as you see it and describe its impact. Present the problem in a nonthreatening, factual manner. Focus on the issue, not on symptoms, personalities, styles or attitudes. Avoid placing blame. Be flexible.

Ask for the other person's views. Keep an open mind, listen carefully and actively, and ask questions as needed.

Restate the problem as you both see it and seek agreement to work towards a mutually satisfying solution. Be willing to own up to part of the problem. Be positive and patient.

Discuss and explore possible solutions. Define the criteria that acceptable solutions must meet. Explore options. Challenge yourselves to come up with alternatives that will satisfy both of you and that will meet the needs or conditions identified. Seek input and offer suggestions. Listen, clarify and acknowledge.

Agree on a solution and define what each person will do to implement it. Make sure that both parties are clear on their responsibilities and assignments. Acknowledge the other person's involvement, cooperation and contribution to the resolution. Agree to meet again to check progress. Adopt a win-win strategy.

Giving and Receiving Feedback

Feedback is the giving of information to a person regarding his or her behavior, actions, approaches, accomplishments and/or performance. If offered at a proper time in an appropriate way, feedback can be a very valuable tool for helping an individual or team achieve improved performance and relationships. High performance teams tend to be extremely effective in both giving and receiving feedback. In these teams, positive feedback is given at least as often as constructive criticism. There is little evidence of the defensiveness that so often characterizes dysfunctional teams.

There are two types of feedback:

- Corrective feedback is given when you want to help someone change and improve.
- Positive feedback is given when you want to reinforce and show appreciation for the way someone behaved or something he or she accomplished.

Corrective feedback is helpful. It encourages the other person to recognize a need and take the actions necessary for improvement. To avoid having the recipient take your corrective feedback the wrong way, it must be presented with care and sensitivity. Your feedback can have a negative impact if:

- It attacks a person rather than an issue.
- It is not related to team performance goals.
- It is inaccurate, exaggerated or sugar-coated.

Feedback can be an essential tool in conflict resolution. It is a way to make an individual aware of a problem or the need for improvement. It can help improve individual or team effectiveness by preventing the build-up of tensions that can result in bursts of anger, damaged relationships and undermined team unity.

At its best, feedback capitalizes on the differences in a team and develops trust among teammates. However, remember that feedback works two ways. In other words, if you want others to accept your feedback in a positive way, you had better be prepared to accept theirs in a similar manner.

Principles of Effective Feedback

Even the most accurate, well-meant feedback might cause the recipient hurt and embarrassment. By keeping the following principles in mind, you can deliver feedback that is both helpful and encouraging:

Make it descriptive rather than judgmental. Focus on what happened, not how you feel about it. Instead of "Your group is doing a lousy job" say, "Output is down 25 percent."

Make it specific, describing in detail what took place. Don't use vague terms. Instead of "You are unreliable," say "Three times in the last two weeks deliveries have been late. The first time was...."

Make sure the feedback takes into consideration the needs of the individual receiving it. You should never give feedback just to get something off your chest. Think about the recipient and put yourself in his or her shoes. Just because something is good for you doesn't mean it is easy to swallow. Make the feedback palatable without making it unrecognizable.

Make sure it clearly describes the impact of the person's behavior or performance in terms of performance, relationships and feelings. Say "As a result of the late deliveries, we have been unable to meet our commitments, and I feel bad about that." Use "I" rather then "you" statements when describing impact or feelings. Instead of "You can't be trusted" say, "I feel that I can't rely on you."

Make sure it is delivered in a timely manner. Feedback is most helpful when it is delivered as soon as possible after a particular incident or event occurs. Remember that it is just as important to catch people "doing right" as it is to catch them "doing wrong." Make sure you don't choose a time when the recipient is preoccupied or distracted or when you're likely to be interrupted.

And, above all, make sure the recipient is the first one to hear your feedback, rather than the last. There is nothing more humiliating than criticism, even constructive criticism, that travels the grapevine before it reaches the person involved.

Make sure it is directed to behavior or performance over which the person has control. In other words, make sure it is targeted to something the person can change. Instead of "You imbecile, you screwed up this week's report again" say, "There are five misspelled words in this week's report and there were three in last week's. Please proofread your spelling more carefully."

Do a check for clarity and understanding. Ask the recipient to rephrase the information you have shared with him or her.

Make sure your feedback is controlled. Don't overwhelm the person with several corrective feedback items that you have saved to unload at one time. Confine your discussion to the one or two most critical items.

Offer alternatives. Be prepared to provide suggestions for improvement if the person asks for them. This is particularly important when dealing with less experienced personnel.

Examples of Corrective Feedback

When delivering corrective feedback, be sure to have a logical plan for the discussion. Consider the following points for structuring the interaction:

State the reason, purpose and importance of the feedback. Relate the feedback to the individual as well as team performance and effectiveness.

Example: "I would like to talk to you about something I have seen taking place in our last several meetings and its impact on our team. Would you like to meet now or would three o'clock this afternoon be more convenient?"

Describe the situation in detail, being specific about the problem, behaviors and their importance. Be specific about the incidents, what was said or done, your reactions and feelings and the potential impact of the person's actions or behaviors. Example: "I may be overly sensitive about this, but in the last three meetings, when I presented information from the quality cross-functional team, I detected what seemed to me to be some cutting remarks. As an example, you referred to the team as 'a bunch of jerks who don't know what they are doing.' I can go on, but the important thing is that our team asked me to represent them on the cross-functional team because of the need to work across the operation on quality improvement. I am trying to keep you and the team informed and get your input, but some of your comments were disruptive and others started to join in. It makes me feel like I am wasting my time."

Clarify details and solicit the other person's views. Ask questions to better understand the reasons behind events. Ask for the other person's view of the situation and listen—empathize if appropriate. Acknowledge the other person's openness and contribution to the discussion. Example: "Can you share your views with me? Can you tell me why you feel that way?"

Obtain agreement that change is needed in order to improve performance, team effectiveness or relationships. Example: "So you feel that I am not the problem, but that other people on the team cannot work toward the best solution. Likewise, you agree that when you feel something is wrong you will bring it out in the open more objectively and not dump on the person involved."

Agree on action to be taken. Seek the other person's ideas for changing his or her behavior or improving the situation. Listen actively, clarify and acknowledge his or her input. Contribute any suggestions you may have.

"What can you do differently in the future so that you can voice your objections and concerns without excessively criticizing one of us?"

Summarize and express appreciation. Check for understanding to be sure both parties are clear about what action will be taken to correct the situation. Express appreciation to the person for being willing to listen and take action.

"I will raise the issue at the next quality team meeting. I'm glad that you will not let things build up and will come to me and share your concerns. Thanks for hearing me out. I know you care about the team."

Receiving Corrective Feedback

Receiving corrective feedback is not the easiest thing to do, especially if it is not being given in a helpful manner. Keep in mind that some people simply don't know how to give corrective feedback. These people may seem rude or belligerent. In reality, they may just be nervous and uncomfortable. Believe it or not, for many people, giving corrective feedback is as hard as taking it. Sometimes people will postpone giving feedback until they have reached a breaking point. By the time they get to you, they will be ready to explode, and will often overstate their case. In either case, keep an open mind and try not to get defensive. Try to look past the behavior and get a real understanding of the problem. Be ready to admit to yourself that the person may have a legitimate gripe. No matter what the initial demeanor of the other person, you can turn most feedback sessions into positive, relationship-strengthening discussions if you:

Listen intently and respond with empathy. Give the person a chance to state his case and present the information to you. Listen for content and feeling. Rephrase, show empathy, encourage him to keep talking, and clarify as necessary. Avoid interrupting and defending your actions at this point. If you allow the other person to talk without interruption and recognize his feelings, he will normally calm down and become more rational and responsive. Example: "I didn't realize it was upsetting to you. I'm sorry. Tell me more about it."

Discuss and clarify details about the situation. At this stage, ask questions to be sure you are clear on the circumstances. It is still too early in the discussion to explain your side of the story. Check for understanding before moving on. Example: "Can you tell me more about how it affected you? Was I the only person doing it? Has this happened on other occasions? Why didn't you come to me sooner?"

Provide information about the situation. This is your opportunity to express your point of view. You may not have been aware of what you were doing or you may have been misinformed about what you were supposed to do. Example: "The memo I received from George seemed to direct that I file the reports directly with him. I didn't realize that I should have cleared them with you first."

Be open to the possibility that you may have been acting inappropriately. Own up to your behavior if that is the case.

Agree on a desired outcome. Find out from the other person how she would like the situation to change or what outcome she is looking for. Example: "Those are my views on the situation. Can you tell me what you want to happen in the future?"

Discuss alternatives and agree on actions that should be taken to achieve the desired outcome. It is helpful for you to ask for suggestions from the other person, listen and acknowledge them and offer your thoughts on what you might do differently in the future. Example: "Now that I realize the problem I have been causing, I need to do something about it. Any suggestions? What should I do if I am not sure on the correct procedure to follow? How about if I spend some more time with you and George to better learn that part of the process?"

Summarize and express appreciation. Check for understanding regarding future actions and thank the person for coming to you about the problem. Recognize the fact that she cares about her job and the team. Acknowledge that you realize she is trying to make things better for everyone. Example: "I am glad we got this out in the open. I know it was difficult for you. I appreciate your help in making the changes we talked about."

Giving Positive Feedback

Giving positive feedback to a fellow team member, customer, supplier, other team, other team member or a helpful support person or resource provider is a very simple thing to do. However, despite the fact that most of us appreciate positive feedback, we overlook or shy away from opportunities to give it. We take for granted that other people know we appreciate their support, cooperation, performance, etc.

Many of the same principles for giving helpful corrective feedback also hold true for helpful positive feedback. Positive feedback is best given when it is descriptive and specific, meets the needs of the recipient, is given with care, states the impact, is timely and relates to actionable behavior. Positive feedback must be genuine and sincere; otherwise, its value is lost.

The purpose of giving positive feedback is to provide recognition and show appreciation. It is a very effective way to encourage the individual to continue with the performance we find beneficial to the team…and to inspire others to follow his example.

In giving positive feedback use the following process:

State the purpose of the discussion and describe the situation. Briefly explain the reason for the discussion so that the recipient has a sense of what the conversation will be about. Example: "Sandra, I want to talk to you about how well you handled the meeting, if you've got a minute."

Describe the behavior and its impact. Describe specifically what the person did, what the results or accomplishments were, and the impact or importance to the team, customer or the organization. Compliment the person as you are doing this. Example: "That was a difficult situation because the other two teams didn't want to cooperate, but you were very skillful in getting them to talk about their problems and concerns. When it was over, we were all one big team. You seem to have the ability to get people to open up and it proved to be helpful. I wasn't sure how the meeting was going to go, but I am glad it went so well. Our performance on the new product launch was suffering because of the lack of cooperation."

Express appreciation and listen to the individual's comments. Expressing appreciation is nothing more than saying things like "great job," "job well done," "thank you," etc. Often this is the extent of our positive feedback, but if it is preceded by a description of the behavior and its impact, it is more meaningful and genuine and effective in reinforcing the right behaviors.

"I am sure the rest of the team is as appreciative as I am. Thanks for taking the lead. It looks like we are over the hump now, thanks to you."

Influencing

Working in teams and having responsibility for managing and improving performance requires making decisions and taking actions. However, this must be done in collaboration with others. That's where the ability to influence comes in handy.

To influence is to use your personal power and interpersonal skills to gain support and obtain resources necessary for achieving results. There will be times when you and your team may need to influence key customers and other groups or may encounter resistance to ideas your team wants to introduce to those outside your team. The more effectively you can influence, the easier it will be to avoid conflict and gain consensus.

When I work with continuous improvement teams or process reengineering teams during their later stages, I often facilitate development of a commitment plan. This is a plan that highlights key individuals whose commitment is necessary in order for the team to implement its plans. After individuals are identified, the team makes a judgment and categorizes the individuals or groups as advocates, helpers, indifferents, or blockers. Once these classifications are complete, the team decides what action is necessary to gain commitment from these individuals. The teams that are most successful in gaining commitment are those with lead individuals who have well-developed skills in influencing people.

When you're trying to influence someone, you may be trying to make that person see the similarities between his or her goals and your goals. Or you may be asking someone to adjust his or her needs in order to support your efforts. For example, you may be working with suppliers to influence them to make changes that will enable your team to better meet customer requirements. You may be working with other teams to obtain needed support and assistance to better meet overall organization needs or to take responsibility for functions and services they provide so your team can extend its domain to better manage a whole process.

Effective influencing requires planning, effective interpersonal skills and a logical discussion process.

Planning

Before approaching someone to influence his or her behavior, you need to prepare for the discussion.
* Identify exactly who it is you need to influence.
* Describe the situation succinctly.

- Identify your immediate goals.
- Define specifically what is needed from the person to accomplish this goal. Mention the value to the team, organization or customer if the objective is accomplished.
- Consider possible objections the person may raise. Use a force-field analysis to identify the objections, resistance, or other hindrances.
- Be open to alternatives. You need to be as flexible as possible. Remember, your concern is the end result, not the means of achieving it.
- Identify others who might be able to leverage your influence.

Select the right time, place and conditions to discuss the situation, and be sure to bring any data that supports your case. Timing is everything. You don't want to hold your meeting immediately after an important event, such as an announcement of layoffs, that may preoccupy the mind of the person you are trying to influence. And don't forget the motto used by everyone from realtors to retailers: Location! Location! Location! That means you don't want to pick a site that is distracting, such as on the noisy shop floor or in the elevator.

Interpersonal Skills

Some people believe that bombarding others with words is an effective way to influence them. I guess the logic behind this theory is that the person on the receiving end of the monologue will eventually give in just to get the speaker to shut up. In reality, however, people are more likely to close their ears—as well as their minds— to a filibuster and simply walk away.

The moral of this story is that there can be no influence without first having a dialogue. Critical information must be gained through questioning, seeking input on options, actively listening, uncovering objections and acknowledging the other person's contributions to the discussion.

Discussion Steps

The following process can be of great help when you are meeting with the person you are attempting to influence:

Clearly explain your purpose and be specific about the action you are requesting. If asking for commitment or support, state the specific actions you believe constitute commitment or support.

Example: " The reason I wanted to meet with you was to get your endorsement for this new improvement we are considering implementing, following a survey we did. I want to review it with you now that we have addressed your original concerns, and have you develop a plan of action including a communication strategy for it within your own business unit."

Succinctly describe the situation, explain your proposal and rationale, explain the benefits of accomplishing your objective and the benefits of the other person's actions. Example: "We have a lot of feedback on problems associated with getting people registered for computer training. Our proposal will provide a formalized procedure for registration. It will make registration easier and more equitable for employees. By implementing this proposal, we should be able to help all business units meet their development needs. Your cooperation and communication will help us get the ball rolling with this new registration process in your unit."

Clarify details about the situation, goal or desired actions. Respond to questions and concerns, and ask questions to obtain additional information needed. Listen actively and check for understanding. Example: "We want to finish implementation of the communication of registration procedures for all business units by the end of the October and have the online pieces of registration completed by the end of the summer. What do you need from us to help you succeed with your information briefings or communication? What else do you need? Does this plan make sense? Any other questions?"

Explore alternatives for achieving the goal. Keep an open mind. Seek ideas for working around objections. Offer your ideas and options. Listen actively.

Example: "Well, if you would want to do a joint effort involving our people, I'm sure we can work it out. What did you have in mind?"

Ensure agreement and clarity by checking for understanding. Acknowledge and express appreciation for participation, contribution and commitment.

Example: "From our meeting today, I will follow up to secure the additional resources you requested by the end of the month. You agreed you would start on the development of the communication plan and give me a call if you have any additional questions. Does that sound correct? Thanks for your commitment to this improvement effort. I'm sure with your involvement and active role in the communication of the registration process the business unit will secure what it needs. Thanks."

Facilitating

Facilitating means removing obstacles or showing the way to a goal. Another role of a facilitator is to recognize team problems and assist the team in addressing and correcting these problems. Every team member can and should facilitate when there is a need. Many teams don't need an external facilitator once the members have developed the necessary combination of interpersonal skills and knowledge of a basic facilitation model. The following is an example of such a model:

Facilitation Model: Do's and Don'ts

A facilitator should not intervene unless there is a problem with the way the group is working, or if there is an opportunity to improve or learn and grow by doing something different.

If the problem or need is not severe, the facilitator will suggest and seek agreement on a course of action. Example: "It seems to me that we have left a couple of members out of the discussion. I would like to hear from them, if there is no disagreement."

If the problem or opportunity is significant, the team should work on the solution as much as possible. Example: "I've noticed over the past few weeks that we have tended to let a couple of our team members decide everything for us. I think we need to talk about it and come up with a way of avoiding this in the future."

When to Facilitate

There are four basic situations that call for a facilitator:

- Task flows for problem-solving or getting the work done are ineffective or can be improved.
- Relationship methods such as supporting or confronting each other are ineffective or can be improved.
- The behavior of one or more members is disruptive or dysfunctional.
- The team appears to have become stagnant and it stops being productive or stops growing in terms of its effectiveness and ability to learn.

Ineffective Workflow Process

Facilitating task flow is nothing more than providing leadership when it is needed. Some of the problems the facilitator may have to help the team solve may include:

- Lack of proper preparation for meetings
- Using ineffective methods during meetings, such as failing to stick to an agenda
- Not following through after meetings
- Omitting critical steps in the improvement process for systematically working on projects
- Inappropriately using tools and techniques
- Failing to use prescribed procedures for planning and scheduling work, determining assignments, etc.
- Not adhering to operating guidelines.

In addition to the situations described above, there may be instances when the team is unsure of how to approach a problem. In that case, the facilitator may be called upon to suggest a process or approach.

Ineffective Relationship Methods

Ineffective relationship methods prevent members of the team from working together as a cohesive unit. Facilitating group relationship issues is nothing more than providing group interaction leadership when it is needed. Ineffective relationship methods can include such things as:

- Unresolved conflicts or ineffective conflict resolution strategies
- Decisions being railroaded rather than being reached by consensus
- Lack of participation or team members who dominate the discussion
- Not valuing or capitalizing on team member differences; treating members as second-class citizens because they are different
- Inadequate discussion; jumping to conclusions
- Conflict within a team or with another team
- Inappropriate use or delivery of feedback
- Lack of listening and respect
- No accountability for decisions
- Not adhering to guiding principles
- Disruptive or dysfunctional behavior

Repeated disruptive behavior by even one individual can seriously affect the functioning of the team. In a dysfunctional team, members may not be owning up to their responsibilities or carrying their share of the load. If not corrected, the dysfunction will spread or create tension and hamper team performance. Included in this category are such behaviors or practices as:

- Withdrawing from group activities
- Dominating team discussions, resulting in decreased member participation and increased frustration
- Being aggressive by attacking, arguing unnecessarily, or lashing out at other members
- Blocking, finding fault, disagreeing excessively, getting sidetracked or making only limited positive contributions
- Clowning around

- Allowing personal problems outside of work to interfere with performance
- Failing to follow through on or complete assignments correctly; not shouldering a fair share of the workload.

Dysfunctional behavior is best addressed in a private discussion in which the facilitator provides corrective feedback.

Team Stagnation

Stagnation or lack of development often occurs because the team is so focused on the task responsibilities that it pretty much ignores the need for team growth. Stagnation may be a naturally occurring and temporary phenomenon resulting from the inherent surge and plateau pattern that is part of the growth process itself. When cross-training is supposed to take place to develop team flexibility, stagnation may occur because of the pressure to get work done. In other words, team members may get so caught up in the work effort that they fail to share information or findings with one another. Or the team may fail to periodically evaluate its relationships and its performance as a unit. It may fail to stop to recognize and reward itself for its accomplishments and work at various points along the way toward meeting its larger goals, making the road to success seem endless and thankless. Whatever the cause of stagnation, it is important that someone on the team recognize it and make it a priority issue for the team to address.

Summing Up

Effective communication skills and the team's ability to manage inevitable conflict can make a major difference in the team's ability to progress and, ultimately, succeed. Leaders and other members must focus on catching and acknowledging people doing the right things as well as on using appropriate techniques when change is needed or when conflict is blocking the team's progression.

As the team progresses from problem resolution to action and implementation, your influence skills will be crucial in maintaining momentum and gaining the commitment necessary to keep moving forward.

In this chapter, I have outlined some of the major methodologies for establishing communication, resolving conflict and using your influence. Look for opportunities to practice the techniques for never-ending improvement.

Workbook Section

Practice

TEAM LEADER

1. Below you will find four statements made by a team member regarding some situation pertaining to the team or team activity. Pretend that the statement is being made to you by another team member. After each statement, write out a reply that uses all of the key interpersonal skills: active listening/rephrasing; questioning/clarifying; empathizing; acknowledging; and seeking. (In real life, you would probably not have to use so many skills in one reply. This is simply an opportunity to practice.)

"When we met with Team B this morning to resolve our differences, they said that they needed better quality from us. How does anyone expect us to do better with the sketchy information we get from Team C, and the incomplete specifications Team B gives us?"

Reply: _____

"I don't know if I am ready to take on responsibility for training the two new people who have just joined the team. I've just gotten comfortable doing all aspects of my current job, and I haven't learned all the jobs yet. What's worse, I've never trained a new member before."

Reply: _____

"I am concerned about getting my part of the project done on time. I am still waiting for the final results from George, and Sarah still hasn't given me the cost information. I've also got my regular work to do."

Reply: _____

"Being on this team has really made a difference for me. I now feel like I have a say and can make a real impact on customers and profits. I don't think I could ever go back to the old way."

Reply: _____

2. Assume you have been assigned to lead a major process reengineering team. You have had several months of data-gathering meetings and are now getting close to making recommendations for large-scale change within the organization. You and other members of the team have noticed one of the members from the sales area withdrawing at times and not being productive or participating. This same individual has also been very vocal in protecting his function, causing a lot of conflict within team discussions particularly as the team has discussed the implications for improvements based on their data collection efforts. You (and perhaps other team members) believe this person may be getting defensive and becomes either withdrawn or hostile at times because he fears losing his job based on the team's proposed reengineering of the business workflows. (This example is actually based on a real-life situation I encountered as an external facilitator.)

Based on this scenario, develop a plan of action. What are the issues? What methods would you use based on your review of communication, conflict and influence techniques? What specific steps would you take and what exactly would you say during your interaction? Test your plan for reactions with other team leaders in your company.

TEAM MEMBERS

This exercise will give you an opportunity to practice giving and receiving feedback. Form groups of three or four. In each group:

One member will practice giving corrective feedback, using the principles for effective feedback and following the discussion steps.

One member will practice receiving feedback, following the steps for receiving feedback.

One member will observe the member giving feedback. The observer will take notes on the discussion steps used and how well the person followed the principles of helpful feedback. Try to record specifically what the person being observed said for each step. After the practice is over, use the notes to give specific, helpful corrective and/or positive feedback to the person observed. Remember to follow the principles for helpful feedback when giving your feedback.

One member will observe the member receiving feedback. The observer will take notes on the discussion steps utilized. Try to record specifically what the person being observed said for each step. After the practice is over, use the notes to give specific, helpful corrective and/or positive feedback to the person observed. Remember to follow the principles for helpful feedback when giving your feedback.

Rotate roles so that everyone will have a chance to practice each role.

NOTE: When in the role of giving feedback, select a behavior, practice, or performance area that is actually in need of some improvement appropriate for the person to whom you will be giving the feedback. Since this is merely a practice exercise, this is a chance for you to try some new and creative approaches. It is also an opportunity to work on a sticky or explosive situation in a safe environment. Pick from the following situations if you can't think of a current volatile situation:

A. Team member is always late in supplying you with data, causing delays for your customers. This team member is very defensive.

B. Team member has an opinion about everything and many members are tired of his pontificating. They want to throw the member off the team because he or she always has to have the last word on everything. This person is not perceived as a team player and rarely seeks the advice or approval of other members on the team for before acting.

C. Team member has some poor personal hygiene habits. You and other members of the team have often found this person's body odor offensive.

Take five minutes to prepare for the discussion, using the corrective feedback steps as your guide for planning the discussion. Decide who will be giving feedback to whom, so that all members can prepare for their practice at one time. There is no need to prepare for receiving feedback. Write the steps on a piece of paper and keep it in front of you to follow when it is your turn to give or receive feedback.

Think of the people you consider effective communicators with good interpersonal skills. Describe the practices and behaviors they use. Do you see these practices and behaviors being used by your team members?

How would you assess the comfort and skill level of your team members in giving feedback to one another? How do team members react when another member is giving them feedback?

Who are the members of your team who seem to be most successful at influencing other team members? What do they do that makes them successful?

Key Tips

If you want to be an effective model on your team, display effective behaviors in both giving and receiving feedback. Look for opportunities to provide positive feedback on a timely basis. Also, be constructive and rational rather than destructive when giving corrective feedback. Most important, don't get defensive when receiving feedback. Use the effective communication techniques described in this chapter.

The key to having an impact is to learn the art and science of influence. Having a plan that outlines what you want to say before your interaction will go a long way toward ensuring your success in gaining commitment and effectively influencing others.

Conflicts are unavoidable. They can be healthy for the team as long as they are resolved. Work toward win-win situations among your team members, using objective problem-solving and seeking mutually satisfying solutions.

9

DECISION-MAKING

All things are difficult before they are easy.
—John Norley

The team has been together for months. The members have been gathering data. They have been analyzing it for problems and improvements. They have looked at every nook and cranny of a process flow chart. They are now ready to develop solutions and plans for implementation. All of a sudden, things change. The team's productivity begins to drop; perhaps turf battles begin to break out. The team is stuck, unable to proceed further; there seems to be a lack of a sound framework to help the group to turn this information into action.

Sound familiar? It certainly rings a bell for me. I have seen it happen many times. Fortunately, this malady is rarely fatal. The group has simply reached a point of indecision.

Remember, most team members are accustomed to having decisions made for them. Gathering information, analyzing and discussing data are pretty familiar tasks for them. But decision-making? That's a whole different story. For many people, the responsibility can feel like preparing to take a high dive into a very small bucket of water.

This is often an issue when company cultures are moving toward empowerment from a history of command and control decision-making. In many of these cases, you find team members who fear they are not ready to make decisions and team leaders who may be reluctant to give up what was considered to be a significant element of their job.

In order for teams to grow and progress, leaders must not only allow but actively encourage the shift of decision-making responsibility to the members. It is they who must determine who should be involved in decision-making. They must be able to recognize when a decision should be made by one member or a subgroup of the team. They should also be able to recognize when making a decision requires a total team effort.

As this transition is being made, the leader's role shifts from primary decision-maker to mentor and guide. It is her job to help the team examine the various types of decisions to be made, figure out how these decisions will be made, and determine what information is needed to make a sound decision.

No one should expect the members of any team to make the transition from decision-followers to decision-makers overnight. The skills needed for effective decision-making must be learned and the responsibility must be earned for both team members and team leader to feel confident and comfortable.

Benefits of Team Decision-Making

Without decision-making responsibility, the team's responsibility for improving and satisfying customer requirements is limited. Empowered teams have the ability to respond more quickly because they don't have to fight through multiple approval processes, overwhelming policies and procedures, unnecessary reviews and checkpoints and other red tape that are so much a part of the traditional bureaucratic structure.

Other benefits of team decision-making are:
- The people closest to the process are in the best position to know what is going on and make necessary on-the-spot, timely, expedient and accurate decisions. This is why the Malcolm

Baldridge National Quality Award and other such honors include among their criteria what the companies offer in the levels of support, training, development and empowerment of customer contact personnel.

The further removed the decision-makers are from the process, the longer it takes to reach a decision. In a highly competitive, changing global economy, speed is one of a company's strongest marketing advantages, while lack of speed can be a fatal flaw.

- The situation is similar to that of an NFL quarterback reading the defense (taking in the latest information) and making adjustments at the line of scrimmage. Can you imagine what would happen if John Elway from the Denver Broncos had to call time out every time he saw the defense changing because he had to have the coach's approval on every decision? Not only would the fans be annoyed, but I am sure a quarterback like Elway would be quite frustrated by his inability to adjust to the defenses and guide his teammates at the line of scrimmage.

- Team members can bring different perspectives and contribute different ideas and approaches to the decision-making process. As the old adage says, "Two heads are better than one." In a cross-functional environment, you have team members who bring varied functional expertise to the table. Often you will find a group of individuals with a wide range of preferences and orientations. For instance, a single team may include creative thinkers, rational planners and just plain doers. All of these different talents and styles can produce positive results if they are working toward common goals and results. When I think about some of the more successful teams I have known, I recall that, in many of them, I found sharp differences in the styles and strengths of the individual members. However, these teams did not see this diversity as an obstacle. They used it to their advantage to achieve great results in decision-making. Research has also shown that a team can outperform an individual, if the full potential of the team is utilized in the decision-making process.

Decision-making responsibility challenges the team and provides opportunities to use members' capabilities that might otherwise go untapped.

Many members of self-directed teams often comment on how much closer and in tune with their teammates they feel when everyone actively participates in the decision-making processes.

I recently took my car to a place in Bucks County, Pennsylvania, called Tire City. In the store, I found the following poem hanging on the wall:

Teamwork Pays Off
Once upon a long time ago,
There was a family of dinosaurs
And a colony of ants.
The dinosaurs ruled the earth.
No living thing could match their
tons of muscle and gigantic size.
One alone would crush a thousand colonies
of ants simply by taking a few steps.
And the ants were powerless to stop them.
But the ants had one thing going for
them—teamwork. Each ant had an important
part to play in the structure of its colony.
Each furthered the riches of the colony in
terms of food and shelter and protection.
The dinosaurs, on the other hand, were loners
—each beast for itself.
Today, dinosaurs are extinct. But ants
are still about, still planning, working,
cooperating with one another for the good of the colony.
Teamwork does pay off.

It is one thing to implement someone else's decision. It is quite another to implement your own. People tend to have a vested interest in, be more committed to, and feel greater ownership for their own decisions. Therefore, team decision-making increases the likelihood of effective implementation. It also makes the team more committed to make any necessary modifications to the implementation strategy until it works. Furthermore, the process of reaching a decision and planning for the decision's implementation provides a far greater understanding of what is involved in effective implementation. This greatly increases the chances for successful implementation.

Effective Decision-Making

Decision-making is a science, not an art. There are certain requirements that have to be met if team members are going to be effective decision makers.

All members must have a clear understanding of who has responsibility for the decision, under what circumstances, and with what limitations or boundaries.

For example, I have often seen improvement teams develop some excellent ideas to improve their companies. After they have spent considerable time reviewing data and have finally arrived at consensus on the best alternative, they are informed that they don't have the budget to implement the idea or that the alternative will have to be studied by the management group in more detail. So, I am not implying that there can't be limitations or boundaries on team decisions. But teams need to be clear about their limitations right from the beginning. Team members and leaders both have an obligation to make sure responsibilities and authority levels are clarified prior to wasting precious time and resources on projects.

Team decision-makers must have information about the situation, alternatives, risks, cause-and-effect relationships and requirements to make an informed decision rather than relying on gut reaction. Often in companies with a real bias for action, teams will begin looking for solutions without first thoroughly assessing the situation or the root cause of problems. As a result, these teams may make quick decisions that only alleviate symptoms rather than solve problems or that consider only the more obvious alternatives rather than the best possible options. At best, the fixes the team develops are merely Band-Aids. Because the root of the problem has not been addressed, it will more than likely flare up again. As a result, the team is so busy putting out fires, there is little time left to try to find permanent solutions.

Information should be readily available to the team in the form of reports, correspondence, and access to databases and information systems. If a pending decision is in a new or unfamiliar area, members should seek information, advice, and input from those who are more familiar with the issue and can contribute to the quality of the decision. A team should never get so close-minded or self-centered that it relies solely on its own information and resources. It is a serious mistake for any team to fail to seek information and input from the team leader, support groups or other experts who may be in a position to help.

Training and experience contribute to a team's effectiveness when making decisions. Many companies use some of the very good formalized training courses that are available about team decision-making. But, like anything else, it's practice that makes perfect. Ongoing use of the decision-making tools and creativity techniques described in this book will help teams grow and develop their decision-making effectiveness. That competence should grow over time as the teams use these techniques in minor or limited situations as their work progresses.

Rookie NFL quarterbacks rarely start games in their first few seasons. If they start out of necessity, the results are often disastrous. On the other hand, if up-and-coming quarterbacks like Brett Farve are groomed, mentored and given experience in controlled situations, they can grow into their role and develop the confidence and experience to be successful.

If a team is given decision-making responsibility, but lacks the authority to execute the decision, it also lacks the true responsibility for that decision. Often, when teams aren't given the authority they need, they get frustrated by the delays and resource constraints that they see as barriers to accomplishing their goals. In such situations the team will probably defer to a higher authority and refrain from making decisions to avoid any second-guessing, changing or reversing of its decisions.

When I am talking to managers about coaching and the need to delegate with authority I often show a John Cleese video on the art of coaching. He shows the frustration of an employee who is not able to learn budgeting skills because her manager hasn't communicated to others the authority this employee has been given to secure resources or remove outdated or inefficient procedures.

The Decision-Making Process

Most successful decision-makers, whether individual or groups, follow a structured process. Even if they're not consciously thinking about the process, it is always there in the back of their minds, guiding them along step by step.

The following is a decision-making model that can help guide your team's progress. When decisions involve the entire team, this process takes longer than if it involves one individual or a small subgroup from the team. When time is short or the decision to be made is one involving low impact or low cost to the company, you may not have the opportunity to use all of these steps. But you should still consider at least some of them, particularly those involving criteria and alternatives. Certainly, when you are making key decisions that have the potential to make a major impact on your company (e.g. hiring decisions or implementing improvements) or decisions that involve high costs or risks, such as installation of a new computer system, you should make sure to follow all of the steps described in the model.

The Decision-Making Model

Step 1.   Define the decision to be made.
Step 2.   Identify criteria to be considered.
Step 3.   Gather and review relevant information.
Step 4.   Identify and analyze alternatives.
Step 5.   Make the decision.

Step 1. Define the decision to be made

What is the objective, issue, change or question requiring the decision? For example, "What type of computer system do we implement?" is not the same objective as "What type of information system do we implement?" In the latter, there may be alternatives beyond computers you might want to consider, such as tele-conferencing and video. The team must have a clear idea about what it is really trying to accomplish with this decision.

Step 2. Identify the criteria to be considered

What are the basic criteria a good decision has to meet? Typical criteria include cost, speed, timeliness, acceptability and minimum disruption or risk. For complex decisions, criteria can be put into two groups: "mandatory"— the decision alternative must satisfy these criteria, and "nice to have"—the team would like these criteria to be met, but it is not absolutely necessary.

For example, if you are purchasing a computer system, there would certainly be some mandatory criteria that would relate to the limit of the number of dollars you are willing to spend or the deadline for implementation of such a system based on the needs of the business. Your "nice to have" might relate to the amount of support for repair, length of warranty, or certain features.

Step 3. Gather and review relevant information

What information will help your team reach a good decision? This may be information the team already knows, information readily available to the team or information the team can obtain from others in the organization (other teams or experts), customers or suppliers. For example, the information needed to purchase the computer mentioned in step 2 might include materials or guarantee information, additional information about systems users might want, data on critical features or background information on training implications of the new systems.

Step 4. Identify and analyze the alternatives

What alternative decisions should be considered? The team should identify, consider, discuss, weigh, and evaluate all possible alternatives.

If members are using the criteria-based decision-making process described in the "Tools and Techniques" chapter, they would gather the data and compare the information about each alternative to see how each stacks up against the mandatory criteria. If some of the alternative computer systems don't meet mandatory requirements, those alternatives can be eliminated. Then the information about remaining alternative computer systems would be compared with the "nice to have" criteria. The best alternative can then be selected using the scoring systems outlined in the "Tools and Techniques" chapter.

Step 5. Make the decision

Discuss feasible alternatives, weigh the pros and cons, consider other factors and make the decision. If it is a team decision, reach agreement and implement it. Decisions can be amended if need be. Although thought, examination and debate are important, they shouldn't inhibit the team's movement like quicksand. Without action, there is no progress.

In our computer purchase example, there may be a couple of alternatives that have received similar scores after they are compared against the "nice to have" criteria. In this situation, the team should also assess the risk. Typically, I suggest that teams discuss risk by imagining they were implementing each alternative and asking what could go wrong. Obviously, the system with the least risk is often the best choice. The team should also consider the "resistance to change" issues that can become barriers to the acceptance of a new computer system or any other innovation.

Decision-Making Styles

Whether you are a team leader or member, there will be times when you will be faced with the questions, "Who should I get involved in this decision?" or "How should I go about making this decision?" These questions call into play your decision-making style.

Decision-making style refers to how many people are involved in making a decision and to the manner in which the decision will be made. Although I am a strong proponent of decision-making by consensus because it tends to get more people involved in and committed to the process, I realize that there are some legitimate reasons for other types of decision-making to occur in companies and on teams. Teams can make decisions in any one of four ways:

Individual. One member of the team makes the decision alone or after conferring with others inside or outside the team.

Minority. Several, but not all members of the team make the decision collectively.

Majority. Everyone is involved, but a simple majority rather than consensus is required to make the decision after discussion. Voting, averaging, or simple "majority rule" techniques can be utilized.

Consensus. Everyone is involved in the discussion, and a decision is reached when all members can agree to support the decision, even if it is not their individual preference. Techniques such as voting, averaging or "majority rule" are not acceptable.

Choosing a Style

A number of factors—including speed, quality, commitment and ownership, involvement, impact, and expertise—should influence who should be involved in decision-making and how the decision should be made.

Speed. How quickly does the decision have to be made? If it must be made on the spot, the person or persons closest to the situation should make it. When speed is the essential factor, one or several members with the needed expertise and information should be involved. Operational decisions usually require promptness, relying on the person(s) closest to the decision point.

Many companies that have successfully used teams to reengineer the way they handle customer service have put computer screens and other technology at the disposal of personnel who directly interact with customers. The result is that as soon as a customer calls, his or her order, complaint or other inquiry can be handled with speed and decisions can be made on the spot. With self-directed teams, decisions can be made faster because customers are not being redirected from one person to another for something that can be handled in a single step, within minutes.

Quality. How important is thoroughness and creativity or originality of thinking? The greater the need for quality, without time constraints, the more important it is that all members be involved and that the decision be made through consensus. Involving a greater diversity of thinkers increases the likelihood that a thorough, creative decision will be reached.

According to an article in the *Journal on Quality and Participation,* the MITRE Corporation formed information technology teams (I-teams) for the specific purpose of sharing information widely across functions and boundaries within the company. In a rapidly changing, information technology-driven world, such sharing is essential for MITRE to stay ahead of the competition. These I-teams bring together different parts of the organization; they find systems effects of actions, policies and projects; and they build strong teams that are more willing to share technology.[1]

Commitment and ownership. What is the degree to which all team members need to feel ownership of and commitment to the decision in order for implementation to be successful? The greater the need for commitment and ownership, the greater the need for consensus. Decisions to alter a process or a major procedural decision require every member's involvement for successful implementation.

One of my key pharmaceutical clients did a very savvy thing by putting together a team to develop an integrated payroll system that involved a number of business units (some recently acquired). The team included people from various functions and all the major business units affected. What made this process somewhat volatile was that many of the units were being paid on different days and at different periods of time (some weekly, some biweekly, etc). As a result of following a step-by-step methodology, gathering key information and ascertaining the need for a wide representation of members because of the decision's impact on the total population, the ultimate decision for the payroll process was agreed to with strong commitment from all parties. It was also implemented throughout the whole company with little resistance. Because it had been made with consideration for all of the issues that pertained to the various business units, all team members took ownership for implementing the process in their own units.

Involvement. What is the extent to which team members feel the need to be involved in decision-making? This depends on the nature of the decision. For example, ordinary operational decisions usually don't require the involvement of every team member. In fact, most members do not care nor do they have the time to be bogged down with every decision.

There are some people on improvement teams who get really excited about mapping a process, and others who prefer not to get into every little detail. The sharp team leader will delegate some of those mapping details to the excited members and get others involved later to help with the final details of the mapping phases.

Impact. Who will be significantly affected by the decision; who will need to be involved? Decisions that impact on other teams, support groups, the team leader, etc., are best made with the other party's input or involvement.

Many successful teams in the later stages of their efforts often find that there are training implications for their improvement solutions. Even if they have a human resource representative on the team, they may bring in specific internal training resources from the company because they know that area will be impacted with many of the decisions the team makes regarding implementation. Obviously, the implementation of your plans will go smoother when you consider who is impacted by them.

Expertise. Who has unique knowledge, experience or expertise and can contribute to the quality of the decision? Some decisions may require more involvement from non-team members, such as engineers, simply because of the need for their expertise.

Types of Decisions and Guidelines for Making Them

How your team chooses to make a decision is usually dictated by the type of decision that it is expected to make. This may sound confusing, but it really isn't. It simply means that some team decisions relate directly to the improvement initiatives they are assigned. Others may be mundane in nature. Teams are generally responsible for decisions in one or more of three areas: *operations, procedures* and *improvements.* The following guidelines should help your team identify the area or type of decision and reach agreement on how each decision should be made by the team.

Operational decisions are day-to-day decisions that need to be made so that products or services produced by the team meet defined requirements.

For example, "Should I shut down or keep running because a key material is slightly off specification, but usable for a lower-grade application?" Or, "We just received a rush order to help a customer with a material problem. When should we switch over to this new order and what should we do about the other orders that are affected?"

The team's charter must be kept in mind when making operational decisions. Individual members can be responsible for decisions pertaining to their assignments, or such decisions can be made by several team members or the entire team.

Operational decisions must be consistent with the team's operating guidelines, procedures and long-range plans. The majority of operational decisions should be made by one or several members; however, if the decision has significant implications, everyone should be involved.

Major improvement recommendations require consensus decision-making. If the team's chartering process is comprehensive enough, it may even specify when all or part of the team may need to be involved in a decision or merely be informed of the decision after it is made.

Procedural decisions involve the way things will be done by the team. These decisions can be divided into three major categories:

• Operational procedures, or operating procedures, define the way in which the work of the team is done.
• Administrative procedures cover such areas as the system for rotating work assignments or the process for planning and scheduling work activities and orders.

- Interaction procedures cover task and group processes that the team has agreed to follow in working together (e.g., ground rules for running meetings).

Procedures guide the team's day-to-day actions and decisions. Rarely do procedural decisions have to be made on the spot. They are typically made by the entire team with full discussion and agreement on the part of everyone. In some cases, the procedure to be followed is a matter of preference and doesn't impact results. That's when simple majority agreement rather than consensus is sufficient.

Improvement decisions concern solutions to problems or changes to better meet the needs of the company by improving process, performance, products or services, or customer satisfaction levels. Improvement decisions are longer-term in nature and require everyone's involvement to obtain commitment and a high-quality decision. Therefore, they are made by the entire team through consensus.

Consensus

Consensus involves everyone on the team. The ability to reach consensus is directly related to the degree to which four conditions have been fulfilled:
- Adequate discussion has occurred.
- Everyone has had reasonable opportunity to influence the other members.
- Everyone has demonstrated a willingness to listen to the views and information offered by the other members.
- Diversity of views and ideas has been sought and valued.

When consensus is reached, all members have accepted and agreed to support a decision. It is a commitment to put forth every possible effort to successfully implement and stand by the decision.

Consensus requires time, the use of all available information, active participation by all team members, effective use of interaction skills, win-win conflict resolution techniques and skills, creative thinking, open-mindedness and group facilitation.

Some organizations believe so strongly in the value of consensus for making major decisions that they state that fact in their basic operating principles.

Except when using the criteria-based selection tool mentioned in Chapter 7, don't base your decisions solely on numbers. Test the team for agreement and disagreement. Play the "devil's advocate" to ensure that all views have been considered before the decision is reached.

The Role-Responsibility Matrix

When the team is developing its original charter (as described in chapter 2, "Team Direction"), it may be helpful to create a basic role-responsibility matrix matching tasks, key roles and responsibilities with members. Later in the team's life, another more complex version of this matrix should be developed. The complexity of the second matrix will depend upon the nature of the team and the scope of its work. For example, an improvement team's second matrix will be a refined version of its first, limited to roles and responsibilities of members within the team. On the other hand, a reengineering team that has already completed its plan may be called upon to develop a new matrix for the entire organization to make it possible for the plan to be implemented.

On the matrix for decision-making, members may be matched with one or more of the following roles and responsibilities:

A = The individual's approval or veto of a decision should be sought

P = A policy-setter for decision-making

S = Gives support or input during the decision-making process

R = A person expected to make recommendations

I = A person who should be informed after the decision is made

Depending on the capabilities of the team and its comfort with decision-making, the team leader may be designated to play any or several of the above roles. The team and its leader should develop a list of responsibility areas and define the roles such as a policy-setter, or a person who makes recommendations for each area. Together, they can then match up roles with people to carry out those roles, based on the members' confidence and the leader's appraisal of the experience level of the team.

Training

Training can be provided in basic decision analysis and decision-making techniques and skills. I often find that training with intact work teams or other improvement teams is best done "just-in-time." In other words, when a major decision has to be made—whether it is a new hire, purchase of a new system or implementation of a new improvement solution—consider combining your training with a real on-the-job application that has meaning to the team.

Team leaders should look for opportunities to turn more and more of the decision-making over to the team so that members can grow and develop the necessary knowledge and skills needed for effective decision-making. During this evolution, the team leader coaches and provides feedback whenever needed to help the team develop and learn.

Probably one of the most important roles of the leader is to provide support as the team learns consensus decision-making, particularly if the team members come from a traditional command-and-control culture. At first, the team may have difficulty adjusting to their decision-making roles and responsibilities. Members may have a tendency to overuse voting and other decision-making tools and techniques only because they are expedient, not necessarily because they produce the highest-quality decisions or ones that foster commitment. The leader should intervene and provide feedback to the group so that all pertinent issues are discussed and all members have their say.

Summing Up

As your team takes on responsibility for managing and improving processes, it should also take on corresponding decision-making responsibility. Turning over decision-making responsibility to a team should be a systematic, evolving process based on the team's readiness and competence.

The benefits of team decision-making are numerous. However, effective decision-making has many requirements, including the use of a rational process.

Although there are many forms of decision-making, consensus, even though it takes time and considerable discussion, will help produce greater commitment during periods of change.

Workbook Section

Practice

Team Leader

Brainstorm a list of improvement decisions your team may be making in the future.

Develop the actual process that should be used to arrive at the decision based on what you read in this chapter.

Using the five-step decision-making process, outline the specifics for each step. Lead a discussion on how you would deal with this as a team, if action had to be taken within the next 30 days. Then discuss how, given more time, you would deal with the typical organization's resistance to change based on your improvement solution.

Review the criteria for decision-making and determine who might be involved in making that decision.

Team Members

Develop a list of responsibility areas for which your team does not currently have decision-making responsibility, but might in the future.

Identify responsibility areas in which you feel comfortable and competent now.

For each responsibility area, identify the responsibility level, the information needed and the source of that information.

Determine who should be involved in making the decision and the most appropriate decision-making style for each area.

Identify those areas you may not have the comfort level or confidence to take on right now. For each responsibility area, identify the things you identified in your answer to the previous question. Identify training or mentoring that would help prepare the team for making these decisions in the future.

Discuss all of the above answers with your leader or manager and jointly develop a plan for the team to take over appropriate decision-making responsibilities in the future.

Key Tips

Clarify the criteria your decision must meet before you go looking for solutions.

Consensus takes time. Make sure you use effective communication skills to arrive at consensus rather than falling back on approaches such as voting.

Take the time to be clear as a team about your decision-making roles and responsibilities. Decide when people need to be informed, more involved in the decision or merely informed after the decision has been made.

Stay focused and rational, always keeping in mind your decision-making steps. This should help manage emotional and defensive responses by team members involved in the decision-making process.

Be sure to introduce some creative techniques into the decision-making process, particularly when the problems are begging for some new, revolutionary solutions.

Take a time-out in your decision-making process whenever it is needed or appropriate. You may be surprised at the innovative solutions you and your teammates can come up with after you have allowed your ideas to incubate overnight.

10

VARIETY IS THE SPICE OF TEAMS

In order to have a winner,
the team must have a feeling of unity;
every player must put the team first,
ahead of personal glory.

—Coach Paul "Bear" Bryant

In the sports world, you constantly hear references to team chemistry and cohesion. This might lead you to believe that team members need to think alike and be alike for the team to be successful. Although there is no question that some degree of commonality is necessary, there is only one way to ensure that a team will be made up of like thinkers: clone all the members. In reality, science isn't quite ready for that. But that's not a bad thing. The differences in experiences, expertise, perceptions and ideas among members are some of the most important assets any team can have.

Have you ever wondered how someone could have a strong opinion about an issue that makes absolutely no difference to you? Or why some issue that is very important to you isn't a top priority for everyone else? The reason is diversity. Whether the differences involve gender, communication styles, personalities, value systems, geography and/or basic individual preferences, variety among members is the spice of life. That is, as long as members can learn to consider all points of view with an open mind and be committed to conflict resolution. A certain amount of disagreement can lead to a lively exchange of ideas resulting in creative solutions and more viable plans and strategies.

A balance of compatibility and differences is essential for any successful relationship, whether that relationship is a marriage, a business partnership or a team. The differences between the partners allow them to complement each other; compatibility gives them common ground.

All human beings share certain common needs. We all need air to breathe, water to drink and food to eat. However, once you get past those basic human needs, people are different in some significant ways.

Some of those differences are readily apparent. Others are subtle, difficult to see at first glance. These differences become more apparent as we live or work together longer. These differences stem from each person's particular background and may be seen in our behavior, capabilities and motivators.

So it's a fact that, in any relationship, differences are going to exist. There's no question about that. The question is, how do we respond to those differences? We can respond in either of two ways:

Differences can be used as justification for excluding people or treating them differently by limiting their roles, ignoring their opinions, discounting their value, working around them or being overly critical of them. In a team environment, this would be a tragic mistake. The team and the organization would be robbed of an extremely valuable resource. Be aware of these tendencies, if they exist, and actively resist them.

The alternative is to value physical, intellectual, and emotional differences and find ways to use the unique capabilities and characteristics of each person. To do otherwise is similar to paying to indulge in an elaborate, exotic smorgasbord, and then selecting only familiar items. Only those who dare to sample the differences are rewarded with the richness the table has to offer.

In the midst of a crisis, who from your team would you want to be by your side?

Why? If you were suddenly in a completely new situation, who would you want to be there with you? Why?

Your answers might be, "Tell me more about the crisis or situation and I will tell you who I would select." However, do you know enough about each individual to make the best selection? Have you been perceptive of the positive aspects and the differences of each team member to know whom to select? For example, which team member would you want to be with if you were:

- Marooned on a deserted Arctic island
- Involved in a car accident in an isolated area and hurt
- Spending a weekend "away from it all" with lots of sports activities
- Teammates, with another person, on a TV game show to win prizes and money
- Held captive by terrorists
- Building a new house by yourself
- Having serious personal emotional problems
- Going overseas to call on a customer
- Assigned to resolve a major process problem in one weekend
- Experiencing major difficulties, as a team, with three other teams—and you, personally, were given one week to resolve those differences and develop a cooperative working relationship.

Most likely, you didn't choose the same team member for each situation. In each instance, did you find yourself choosing from among the same small group of individuals? Do you know enough about the other members to accurately include or discount them? If you aren't sure, it is probably time for you to learn more about the differences and the skills, knowledge and expertise that various team members bring to your team.

Individual differences need to be recognized, accepted, valued and tapped for maximum team performance. First, we need to recognize the sources and nature of the differences. Second, we need to affirm those differences and find ways to use each team member's uniqueness to the entire team's advantage.

When I think about variety and differences, I don't have to go any further than my own family. I have two sons. My oldest, Michael, 19 years old and studying to be a computer animator, is very analytical and detailed in nature. It takes him forever to make a purchase decision. You should have been with him during his numerous trips to find his first car! Talk about analysis paralysis! Then I have my younger son, Jeffrey, age 16, the fast talker in the family. He doesn't have a clue what paying attention to detail is all about. Michael is so intense he even puts his paper clips in order in the desk drawer, but when you walk into Jeffrey's room you think a tornado just came whizzing through. When I get that detailed, gritty work that requires detail like overhead transparencies for my presentations, I sometimes consider Michael as a resource (at least when he is home from college) because he not only has the skills but also the inclination for the type of work I need completed. Jeffrey more often comes to mind for chores of a looser, more general nature such as cutting the grass or going to the store.

Ways of Looking at Differences

We are all from different backgrounds. We are all unique as a result of when and where we were born and the experiences we had while growing up. Other differences may stem from gender, the geographical region in which we were raised, the geographical areas where we have lived, our ethnicity, our religion, and our cultural heritage. My cousins at one time called me the city slicker. I called them country bumpkins. Now we all live in the suburbs.

There is a tendency to stereotype people based on their background. However, we need to avoid stereotyping and, instead, learn to expect and accept differences. Stereotyping means making assumptions—and that causes us to see someone as we think they should be, or, perhaps as we want them to be, instead of who they really are.

Differences in the way we are can stem from our earliest days as children. How we were raised and educated and with whom we interacted can affect three concrete areas that make people different: drivers or motivators, capabilities and approaches. Your background helped shape your values and views. They played a part in determining what motivates or drives you. It manifests itself in your capabilities and your style or preferred way of approaching things both in life and in work.

Motivators

The first area of differences that we can assess is what motivates peoples. Motivators are the sum total of the values, views, beliefs, aspirations, desires, likes and priorities held by an individual. They are the things that turn on the energy valve inside each one of us, that gets the heart pumping, the adrenaline flowing and the mind racing. Like our differences, many of our motivations are formed during our earliest childhood years. Based on research conducted by noted psychologists Abraham Maslow[1] and David McClelland,[2] people may be motivated by a number of basic needs. These needs are:

Assurance. The need is for order, structure, security, stability and predictability. People who buy a great deal of insurance or who drive Volvos may fall into this category. Many times, these people are the team members who find change the most difficult and are often perceived as the low risk-takers in the group.

Affiliation. The need is to belong and to be accepted by our peers for companionship, harmony and group identity. You have probably noticed some of your colleagues or friends who thrive on being involved on teams at work or social events. They are always attuned to the little things that they associate with close friendly relationships. They become concerned when someone forgets to stop and say hello in the morning. They like to engage in a little small talk before getting down to business. They get turned off when others don't take time to relate and interact.

Achievement. The need is for accomplishment, recognition, results and opportunities to demonstrate their competence to others. Quite frequently, these people are self-starters—all you have to do is give them the numbers and the resources to get the job done and their energy valves will drive their behavior towards results. These people are goal-oriented. We see many of these individuals in research and other areas requiring innovative solutions because they are driven to make significant contributions to society, such as curing a major disease or some social ill.

Power. The need is to exert influence and to make an impact. These people tend to like autonomy. They like to have the freedom to experiment and take risks. People motivated by the need for power can often be valuable team members. They may be very successful when it comes to introducing change and gaining commitment from others to buy in to the team's solutions.

Self-actualizing. These individuals have a powerful self-awareness and a willingness to make choices for themselves. They are independent, yet they show a deep caring for and honesty with themselves and others.

Don't try to figure out which is the best category in which to classify yourself or your team members. There isn't one. And that's the whole point. But it is important to recognize that people react and respond to the same situation and conditions in different ways depending on which motivator is the strongest for them. It is also important to recognize that, in some cases, a person's key motivation can change over time. So don't think that just because you have identified a person's key motivator at one point in time you have him or her pegged for life.

As you appeal to other team members, think about their style. What motives can you identify? Do they typically seek more influence and control in situations? Or are they analytical types who are only persuaded by numbers? Do they concern themselves with interpersonal relations within the company? In other words, if you expect to deal effectively with people, don't just tell them what's good for you; figure out how it's also good for them. It's awfully hard to push people to do something; it's much more effective to motivate them.

Capabilities

Capabilities refer to the sum total of a person's skills, knowledge, abilities and competencies. Capabilities can be physical, emotional or intellectual. They typically involve social, technical or administrative areas.

Social capabilities involve effectively working with and leading people as individuals and as groups.

Technical capabilities relate to the performance of job-related tasks. In the case of a team studying software improvements, a technical capability might involve being able to review and study various software packages and updated systems enhancements.

Administrative capabilities relate to the management or coordination of work and improvement activities. The ability to run effective meetings is an example of an administrative capability.

Every team should work to understand the capabilities of its members in the earliest stages of start-up so that the team has an understanding of its strengths as well as areas of potential development. Often in ad hoc improvement or reengineering teams, the team leader may initially outline some of the major capabilities needed on an improvement project (sometimes referred to as a skill and knowledge matrix or team training needs assessment). Then the names of team members will be highlighted along the top of the assessment, and check marks noting those people with the needed capabilities will be placed next to their names. This document serves as a developmental planning tool for members who may need to refine or develop in areas where the team needs additional depth.

Once you have a sense of the team's capabilities, you can begin using each member to make contributions based on their particular areas of strength. Keep in mind, however, that your team is not limited to the resources its own members can provide. Your analysis will also help show your team where other people outside the team might be able to make valuable contributions to the team's effort.

Approaches

In the mid-twentieth century, a prominent Columbia University psychologist named Dr. William Marston (*Emotions of Normal People*, Persona Press, 1928, 1979) popularized the concept of temperament as a tool for understanding oneself and others.

One of the assessment instruments I use vividly demon-strates the four basic behavioral types that Dr. Marston identi-fied. These temperament types are usually classified as D, I, S, and C, which stand for dominance, influencing, steadiness and conscientiousness.*

Our individual temperament greatly influences the way we approach or deal with situations. The following nine different aspects of life and how people approach them should give you a clearer understanding of this concept:

Approach to Work. Are you primarily concerned with merely getting a job done or doing it well? A tendency for getting immediate results versus ensuring quality and accuracy bring different value-added dimensions to your team. It also could influence your decisions relating to key roles and assignments.

Approach to Learning. Do you learn by trying to understand underlying concepts or do you learn by doing? When I facilitate group sessions on coaching approaches, I often use an exercise in which I have participants build a simple object such as a cup. To begin the exercise, I read directions on how to build the object. Then I hand out written details. I finally give them a picture of how to assemble the object. It is interesting to see how some individuals succeed in the exercise simply by listening and hearing the direc-tions. A larger number of people need step-by-step written instruc-tions before they are able to construct the object. Many others are more visual and need to see a picture of the object they are attempting to assemble. Finally, some people learn best through trial and error.

Which one of these is your preferred approach? When trying to explain something to another member of the team, have you considered the possibility—more likely the probability—that this individual's approach to learning may be different from yours?

Approach to Thinking. Do you tend to follow a structured thought process or do you tend to think of things in unusual and novel ways? There is merit to many approaches and value in both

---

*Information on behavioral tendencies is also based on information found in the Personal Profile System® published by Carlson Learning Company.

rational and creative approaches to thinking at various stages of your team's projects. The rational thinkers may be great at analyzing problems and extracting meaning from tons of data. The creative thinkers are often great at taking information and developing new and creative plans and strategies for solving problems. Try to identify the preferred approaches of your fellow team members. Are you using the diversity of your team to its fullest advantage?

Approach to Understanding. Do you rely on gut feel or logic? Often the logical types can help ensure that the team has consensus on the root cause of a problem before it jumps into action. Remember, if your team doesn't accurately identify the root cause of a problem, it usually solves only symptoms, not the core problem itself. So use those logical thinkers to help keep your team on track.

That doesn't mean you should ignore the input of members who rely on gut instinct for understanding. These members can help the team assess the risks inherent in any solutions that may be proposed. Allow the gut instincts of these members to help your team avoid or at least be prepared for obstacles that may stand in the way of implementing any new solutions.

Approach to Life. What is your overall outlook on life? Do you expect things to work out or do you tend to expect problems? Don't ignore the devil's advocates among your team members, but, at the same time, make sure the voices of optimism are heard as well. It is this balance that results in a team that proceeds with a well-thought-out plan and an expectation for success.

Approach to Working with Others. Do you tend to take control of or support others? Count on the dominant types to accept challenges, solve problems and help the team get results. Just as important are the steady types who can be relied upon for support and cooperation in carrying out tasks.

Approach to Influencing. Do you attempt to influence the actions of others by persuading or pushing? When we look at influence research, we know that push works in some instances, but, in some cases, a more indirect approach using a pull or persuasion strategy may prove to be more effective.

Approach to Communicating. Do you tend to be the talker or the listener in a conversation? While one of these styles may be preferred, perhaps you need to consider being more flexible and adapting to the style of each member on your team. Some talkers might have to stop and listen to be effective, while some listeners may need to "step it up a notch" and take the lead once in a while. Sometimes our preferences get us stuck in our own style and interfere with our effectiveness. Our communication approach may be one of the easiest approaches to try to change when the situation warrants.

Approach to Dealing with Change. When changes take place, do you get energized, or traumatized? If many of your team members are of the "steadiness" or support orientation described in approach 6, you may need others who can react quickly to unexpected change.

Summing Up

Variety is truly the "spice" of teams, keeping member interactions lively, creative ideas flowing and progression steady and on course. Capitalizing on differences among team members may require some change of mindsets and a number of very deliberate actions, including the following:

Accept that differences exist and are healthy.

Discover, better understand, accept and inventory the differences that exist among your team members.

Affirm the value of team members' differences by forming five new habits. By affirming members' contributions and strengths, you will encourage them to share those strengths with the team. Also, be sure to affirm team members' attempts to consider the diversity of others and to develop flexibility.

Make it a habit to build others' self-worth. Be quick to praise, express confidence in their abilities, acknowledge their uniqueness and contributions, respect their differences and reinforce their willingness to be different.

Make it a habit to listen to others for better understanding. Listen intently, listen before talking, listen to learn, and encourage them to express themselves.

Make it a habit to ask questions to learn what someone is saying and to better understand his or her viewpoint. Ask for information, opinions, clarification and understanding.

Make it a habit to seek others' ideas and input before offering your own.

Make it a practice to maintain objectivity by focusing on issues rather than on individuals. Don't let personality or motivational differences cloud the issue; don't assume that everyone sees the issues the same way you do. Expect differences.

Workbook Section

Practice

TEAM LEADER

Read the following list of motivators and examples of character traits. Circle three or four motivators that most closely represent your nature.

Motivators: *Examples:*

Accomplishment: I like setting and working toward goals.
I take pride in my work.
It is important to me that our team accomplishes its goals.

Attention: I like others in the organization to see my work.
I don't mind being the center of attention.
Recognition from others means a lot to me.

Autonomy: I enjoy the freedom to decide how to do my work.
I don't mind working on my own.
I rarely feel the need for supervision or instructions.

Challenge: The more challenging the work, the more I like it.
I like to take on the tough jobs or assignments.
I need to feel that the work I do is important.

Clarity: I do my best work when I know what is expected.
I work better when procedures are well-defined.
I work best when instructions are provided.

Camaraderie: Being part of a team is important to me.
                I like working closely with teammates and
                    other teams.
                Relationships are very important to me.

Competence: I welcome opportunities to sharpen my skills.
                I get satisfaction from training other people.
                I look for ways to change and improve
                    myself.

Encouragement: I prefer working with a coach or instructor.
                I appreciate encouragement from other team
                    members.
                I perform best when there is not too much
                    pressure.

Expertise: I like to be known as an expert by my peers.
                I appreciate being recognized for my skills
                    and abilities.
                I welcome people asking me for my advice.
                I welcome opportunities to learn new things.
                I enjoy making decisions.

Harmony: I try to accommodate the opinions and
                    desires of others.
                It is important that team members agree as
                    much as possible.
                I do what I can to smooth things over and
                    maintain good working relationships.

Order: I like having a system to accomplish tasks.
                I work better when routines are stable.
                I work best when there are no sudden
                    problems.

Stability: I don't like a job that has too much variety.
                I need time to adjust to change.
                I perform best with few changes to
                    accommodate.

Supportive: I am open to advice and suggestions from others.

I try to meet the expectations of my team members.

I am willing to follow the leadership of others.

Variety: I like to have a wide range of responsibilities.

I like to perform different jobs and rotate assignments.

I welcome changes in priorities or procedures.

2. Review the following capabilities assessment. Rate yourself in the capabilities listed using the following scale:

1 = significant improvement needed
2 = improvement needed
3 = average
4 = strong
5 = very strong

Capability   **Assessment**

SOCIAL CAPABILITIES

Leading groups   _____

Selling proposals and influencing others   _____

Communicating   _____

Resolving conflicts   _____

Obtaining support and cooperation   _____

Humor   _____

Working with others   _____

Supporting others   _____

ADMINISTRATIVE CAPABILITIES

Planning and scheduling   _____

Solving problems   _____

Understanding complex concepts   _____

Coordinating   _____

Presenting   _____

Organizing   _____

Creative thinking   _____
Collecting information   _____
Writing reports, memos, proposals   _____
Analyzing information   _____

Technical Capabilities

Training others   _____
Learning new things (job knowledge)   _____
Learning new jobs   _____
Following instructions and procedures   _____

Team Members

Using these two exercises, identify your three or four main motivators and strongest capabilities. Review your findings with other team members. Seek feedback from other members to obtain their viewpoints. Discuss how the team can use the strengths of each member to develop and strengthen other members.

After validating your results with others, identify three areas where you could use development. Seek validation from the team members. Ask them how they might support you with your developmental plans.

Discuss the nine approaches in the chapter. Have team members volunteer and identify their preferences. Discuss how the preferences could help the team or hinder the team.

Individually, develop an action plan based on the entire discussion on the variety within the team.

Key Tips

Be aware of the variety that exists within your team. Take advantage of what that diversity offers your team and how it can assist the team in achieving its goals.

At the launch of your team, take stock of the members to ascertain the team's strengths. Use this assessment to produce a developmental plan to help the team grow stronger.

It's not a bad idea to use some personality type gauge early in the team's development to ascertain preferences within the team. This is a common team-building intervention that can help members understand their differences so they can communicate more effectively with one another.

Be aware of individual differences in your attempts to communicate and influence various team members. Don't get stuck in your own preferred style. You may have to stretch to be effective with different people on the team.

Consider the differences among the team members as you plan interactions with them on a one-on-one basis. You are more likely to be successful in your interactions with others and in maintaining a motivated environment.

11

MOVING AND DEVELOPING:
TEAM STAGES

*Quality is never an accident; it is always the result of high
intention, sincere effort, intelligent direction and skillful
execution; it represents the wise choice
of many alternatives.*

—Willa A. Foster

It was the early 1980s. As I entered the classroom, I wondered whether I really wanted to be involved in this program at a local university. This particular course was something called a T-group, a training group; it was about group dynamics.

As I sat down, I could tell this was no ordinary class. Chairs were set in a disorderly fashion around the room. There didn't appear to be any appointed instructor for the program. Minutes went by (it seemed more like hours) before someone announced, "I'm your professor." That was all she said. Somewhat uneasily at first, the group started to get to know one another. Occasionally the woman claiming to be the professor would utter a one-word sentence. We proceeded in this unstructured—and totally unorthodox—format for most of the two condensed weekend sessions of the program.

After the initial honeymoon period, when everyone in the group was on his or her best behavior, one of the members, a lawyer, began to make certain pronouncements that seemed to spark conflict. Signs of a power struggle began to appear. Some arguments about religion, sex, and even race turned into outright battles. This continued throughout the first weekend into the second. Eventually most of the group turned against the attorney and a few others. It got pretty ugly for a while.

Then the group stopped arguing and began talking in the hope of reaching an understanding. We knew there had to be a method to all this madness and we all agreed that we wanted to get some benefit from these sessions. We set a goal: we would work together toward understanding the significance of what we had experienced at the sessions.

Soon the environment became more positive and hospitable. People had gotten to know each other a little better and began addressing each other more on a more personal level. The group increasingly engaged in more productive behavior. As we approached the end of the session, the creative juices were flowing. We seemed to be actually enjoying this experience.

It wasn't until I had a chance to reflect on the experience later that I realized I had gone through what many of you have experienced in your past teams—stages of team development. These stages, if acknowledged and understood, can help explain team situations and why a team may feel or behave in a certain way at a particular moment in its existence.

You can also observe these stages of development in sports teams. First, there's the quite civil and calm "getting to know you" stage. As the players become more familiar with one another, conflicts are likely to emerge. These conflicts may be over leadership, goals, roles or any number of other issues. They may manifest themselves as undercurrents or blow up into all-out struggles.

Eventually, the dust settles. Members start focusing on the job at hand. This is the stage during which the team exhibits high performance, lots of synergy and plenty of feedback. Members on the team are really tapping into each other's strengths.

Teams, like the individual human beings they are made of, go through predictable stages of development similar in many respects to childhood, adolescence, young adulthood and adulthood. At times, growth and development can be painful and slow. But growth and development does happen—given the right environment.

In the early stages, the team leader's role is to provide opportunities for learning and an environment that promotes growth. Eventually the team will mature to the point that the leader, just like a parent, is needed more for advice and support than for decision-making and task assignment.

Understanding the stages teams go through can make it easier for members to ride out the early rough times, accelerate the team's development at any time or rejuvenate the team spirit, productivity and progress during the later stages.

Stages of Development

A team can expect to progress through four stages of development, if it stays together long enough. These stages include start-up, struggling, stabilizing and soaring.

Stage 1: Start-up. This is the childhood stage of a team. There is so much to learn, to master, and to accomplish. It is a period of discovery. It is a time of excitement, great expectations and more than a little apprehension.

Stage 2 : Struggling. Just as adolescence can be a rough time, this is a rough period for a team. By this time, the realities of life have become apparent. Members have come to realize that things are a lot more difficult than they had first appeared to be. The team may experience some hard knocks as members learn new skills and take on new responsibilities. This is also a time for developing and struggling with relationships. It is a time when members begin to question their competency, their authority figures and each other.

Stage 3 : Stabilizing. The worst is over. Self-confidence and self-esteem are on an upswing and the future seems more sure and positive. The team, like a young adult, has come to terms with itself. There is a new focus on performance, accomplishment and the mission and goals of the team. Healthy, longer-term relationships are being established—a can-do attitude is developing.

Stage 4 : Soaring. The team has reached maturity. Members are working together and performing well. There are opportunities to grow and develop as the team accepts challenges and handles changes.

It is important to understand that these stages of team development are normal. Team members, therefore, should have realistic expectations from the beginning. As much as team members and the team leader would like to see the team soar from the beginning, it is unreasonable to expect it.

Understanding these stages of development enables the leader and members to always focus on the current stage and determine what actions and improvements the team can make to ease its movement to the next stage. Each stage of development represents a potentially higher level of effectiveness and performance for the team.

The progression from one stage to the next is not necessarily linear, however. It is not unusual for the team to reach a plateau for some time. After the fourth stage, soaring, the team's development does not end. Learning and development never stop. Opportunities to be more effective and to achieve higher levels of performance are always imminent.

Like many other things in life, development can go backward as well as forward. Events and changes can take place that may cause the team to revert to an earlier stage, for a brief period, until the team realizes what has happened and takes steps to move forward.

Some causes for backtracking in the team's development are:

When new members are added or replace former members, a new team is formed and earlier stages of development are repeated. However, the team often matures at a faster pace the second time around.

A significant change in business conditions and management's response to that change can stress the team and cause it to slide backward. For example, a change in the organization's mission, products or services, owners or key team members (team leader or team manager) will alter the organization's internal environment—producing stress on the team and affecting its stage of development.

Like a tree that experiences a loss of nourishment or a machine that is not maintained, a team can deteriorate due to lack of attention and maintenance. Lack of organizational support and reinforcement, lack of training and development, lack of information and/or loss of alignment with the organization's vision, mission and direction can cause a team to lose ground.

Stage 1: Start-up

In this stage the team is in the start-up mode. Members are making the transition from an individual to a team orientation and are becoming familiar with one another and the mission of the team. At this stage, the team may appear to be working effectively and making progress with its activities. Camaraderie is developing among team members. At this stage, all this harmony is only skin-deep, however, and will be challenged as problems and issues begin to rise.

I see many teams at this start-up stage, particularly in companies that extensively use ad hoc temporary teams. For project (either cross-functional or virtual in nature), process improvement or reengineering teams, success at this stage can be very critical because the team is often pulling together associates of the company who haven't worked with one another on such an intensive level in the past.

Characteristics of Teams at Start-up

Feeling excitement and pride about being part of something new.

Experiencing anxiety about goals and what it will take to accomplish them.

Being suspicious, fearful, and anxious about the organization's expectations for the team.

Sensing anxiety and uncertainty about one's own role and ability to contribute. Members may be wondering, "What's my role? Where do I fit in?"

Feeling eager, with high expectations and optimism.

Seeking orientation and information about goals, roles and direction.

Finding that productivity is low, but morale is high.
Constantly learning and discovering.
Getting to know other team members.
Becoming familiar with tasks.
Depending on the team leader.
Attempting to determine acceptable behavior and how to deal with group problems.
Establishing individual and team identity.
Testing each other's views.

Activities of Team Members in Start-up

Learn about tasks and skill requirements.
Get to know team members—including their skills, capabilities and expectations.
Define tasks, activities and roles.
Outline team goals and direction.
Create structure, such as methods, procedures, rules, etc.

What the Team Can Do to Help Itself

Don't try to take on all tasks and responsibilities at once.
Focus on technical issues and task processes.
Focus on small, simple projects to learn skills, develop confidence, and obtain a sense of accomplishment.
Learn about and question everything for a better understanding.
Do some team-building to lay the groundwork for effective relationships.

What the Leader Can Do to Help the Team

Promote the team's understanding of the organization's broader vision, mission, guiding principles and expectations.
Support the team in developing its mission, guiding principles, operating ground rules, logistics and mechanics.
Assist team members in recognizing team and member responsibilities, roles and activities.

Stage 2: Struggling

In the struggling stage, the team is recognizing and confronting issues. Team members are beginning to realize the enormity and challenge of their objective. Members are becoming impatient with the apparent lack of progress and are questioning one another's commitment and contributions. Some members begin to push for change while others resist it. Most likely, there is widespread dissatisfaction.

This stage may set in soon after a team's start-up. Struggles often develop over power, roles or goal direction. I see this often and am called in to deal with some areas of team conflict. Teams can stay in this stage for months if there hasn't been much clarity about goals or ongoing communication to the team regarding expectations. I have also seen this develop into a lengthy stage if some high achievers on the team feel that some members are not contributing and are not committed to the team's goals.

Characteristics of the Struggling Stage

Feeling frustrated and impatient over the lack or slow pace of progress.

Being angry with each other for rejecting opinions, views and ideas.

Becoming impatient with members who don't appear to be pulling their own weight.

Experiencing frustration and anger related to goals, activities and tasks.

Feeling incompetent.

Having negative feelings towards and dissatisfaction with the team's dependence on the leader.

Competing for control and breaking into factions.

Recognizing a gap between original expectations and reality.

Dominating by some members and withdrawing from participation by others.

Arguing and defensiveness.

Lacking appreciation for members' differences.

Finding that productivity and morale are low.

Wanting to resort to former ways of doing things.

Getting to know each other.

Feeling confusion, anxiety, pressure, and stress related to new or additional responsibilities.

Testing other members' commitment.

Activities of Team Members in the Struggling Stage

Redefine goals, roles and tasks.

Raise issues and bring them into the open.

Learn how to work together.

Develop interaction, conflict resolution and feedback skills.

Revisit vision, mission, principles and operating guidelines.

Develop performance measures and monitor performance.

What the Team Can Do to Help Itself

Use task and group interaction skills.

Practice understanding, valuing others and capitalizing on differences.

Assess effectiveness and develop plans for improvement.

Work at improving team members' effectiveness in using tools and techniques for improvement, problem-solving and decision-making.

Be more willing to share information and disclose feelings and concerns in a positive and helpful manner.

What the Leader Can Do to Help the Team

Confront unproductive or dysfunctional behavior.

Encourage openness, honesty, interaction, feedback and conflict resolution.

Advocate that the team continue with the techniques for improvement, problem-solving, and decision-making.

Stage 3: Stabilizing

In this stage, members begin to accept the team and their roles and responsibilities in it; the other members and their differences;

and the mission, guiding principles, ground rules and goals of the team. Competition is replaced with cooperation and the team begins to handle conflict productively. The team becomes better organized, more creative and finds more effective ways to achieve its goals.

You often see this phenomenon in sports teams. The television stations will publicize the bickering or infighting going on between team members or members and coaches, and before you know it, the team seems to suddenly snap out of its battles and starts performing consistently well together.

Characteristics of the Stabilizing Stage

Valuing differences in needs, capabilities and approaches.
Recognizing newfound experts for their expertise.
Finding it more comfortable to work together.
Feeling a growing sense of trust.
Experiencing a greater sense of accomplishment and self-confidence as a result of the team's progress.
Being more willing to give and receive feedback.
Resolving conflicts through win-win solutions.
Being willing to seek and use each other's ideas.
Growing willingness to operate according to guiding principles and operating guidelines.
Increasing harmony, support and commitment to each other and the team.
Beginning to develop shared leadership.
Improving morale and productivity.
Beginning to think in terms of "us versus them."

Activities of Stabilizing Teams

Develop shared leadership.
Further develop and share skills and knowledge.
Evaluate team task and group interaction effectiveness.
Redefine goals, roles and tasks.
Develop relationships with other teams, support groups and resource providers.

What the Team Can Do to Help Itself

Cross-train and use team experts to develop other members.

Capitalize on the unique capabilities of each team member.

Develop win-win conflict resolution practices.

Perform a critical and constructive evaluation of team task and group interaction effectiveness.

Develop devil's advocate thinking to compensate for harmony-preserving group thinking.

Develop facilitation skills.

Make extra efforts to reach out and strengthen contacts and relationships with customers and suppliers, other teams, resource providers and other experts.

What the Leader Can Do to Help the Team

Relinquish control and encourage leadership from within the team.

Become more of a coach and advisor.

Involve the team with other teams and organizational units in cross-functional and organization-wide issues.

Begin to expand team decision-making responsibilities.

Encourage team self-facilitation.

Review and provide feedback on team performance data.

Stage 4: Soaring

In this stage, the team works together effectively and performs well. Members are comfortable with their respective roles and have learned to use differences to the team's advantage. The team is also clear and comfortable with its purpose and relationship with other parts of the organization. At some point in time, the team will begin to think strategically and look for ways to expand its domain and responsibilities depending on its charter and longevity.

I'm sure you can think of a team at this high-performance stage. I think of the sports dynasties such as the New York Yankees, the Green Bay Packers or Pittsburgh Steelers, UCLA during its run in college basketball or the old Montreal Canadiens. All of these teams were consistent winners. Some of you may have spotted a soaring team in music, in work environments or some other hobby or personal pursuit.

Characteristics of the Soaring Stage

Solving problems individually and collectively.

Having a sense of unity and closeness.

Understanding clearly defined and recognized roles and capabilities.

Maintaining close links with customers, suppliers, other teams, resource providers, support groups and cross-functional teams focused on customer needs and organizational goals.

Encouraging, supporting, and reinforcing other team member's opinions and actions. Members know they can count on each other.

Feeling fully committed to the team, its mission and goals, and the broader goals and direction of the organization.

Experiencing satisfaction, pride, excitement and enjoyment associated with being part of an effective, successful, high-performing team.

Using effective task and group processes.

Sharing leadership.

Seeking ways to improve and expand the team's capabilities and contributions.

Experiencing high morale, productivity and performance.

Practicing effective interaction, feedback, conflict resolution and influencing skills.

Being proactive and responsive to changes coming from the external environment.

Activities of the Soaring Stage

Expand areas of task responsibility to improve efficiency, reduce errors and improve overall performance.

Continuously improve products and services, process performance, team performance and team effectiveness.

Assume day-to-day decision-making responsibilities.

Prepare for additional human resource and management responsibilities such as selection and performance evaluation, budgeting and facilities planning.

What the Team Can Do to Help Itself

Use measurement, evaluation and feedback to make necessary changes to maintain and improve performance and team effectiveness.

Confront and resolve team task and group interaction issues promptly.

Use the leader and other organizational resources for learning and development.

Develop and refine individual and team skills to improve effectiveness, performance and flexibility.

Identify additional decision-making responsibilities, other areas of task responsibility and areas of human resource or management responsibility.

Ensure that members have the training and information needed to assume these responsibilities.

What the Leader Can Do to Help the Team

Allow the team to function independently, serving as its own coach, trainer, advisor and process consultant.

Provide direction, information, training, resources and authority so that the team can manage day-to-day responsibilities and implement improvements.

Offer support, information, training and opportunities for the team to take on increased responsibilities.

Manage the boundaries and keep the team well informed on organizational issues and direction.

Stellar Teams

At one time or another, you may have known of—or, if you were really fortunate, been associated with—a particularly effective, productive team. It's also possible that you have had the experience of being on an ineffective, unproductive team. Think about some of the differences between the two. What were the characteristics, practices and behaviors associated with both types of teams?

Characteristics of Stellar Teams

An effective or stellar team is defined by benchmarks in:
Purpose
Roles and responsibilities
Leadership
Methods, processes and procedures
Interaction and communication
Talents and capabilities
Climate or team environment
Intergroup relationships

Use these criteria to periodically assess your team's effectiveness and performance.

Purpose. The mission, direction and goals of the team are clearly defined, understood and accepted. Members are committed to and working toward accomplishment. Most successful teams that rise above the others have clear focus on goals. Some improvement teams I have facilitated have been apprehensive about what change might mean to them. When that happens team leaders can be extremely valuable. To ease team members' apprehension, gain their commitment and increase the likelihood of their success, team leaders should have a clear set of guidelines from sponsors or steering committees. They should also allot ample time for discussing the purpose, strategy and specific goals and to develop consensus around them prior to proceeding into the major work of the project or improvement initiative.

Roles and Responsibilities. Roles and responsibilities for work activities and team processes are clearly defined, understood and accepted by the team. Members seek ways to rotate and expand responsibilities to increase flexibility and the team's contribution to the organization.

A stellar team builds strength by rotating roles and responsibilities such as running meetings, taking notes, being a scribe at the flip chart or talking to key influencers in the organization.

Nonstellar teams have people bumping into each other in confusion over their roles and responsibilities.

Leadership. Leadership from within the team is effective and shared by all members, if the situation and their capabilities warrant it. A team may become frustrated when an obviously capable person continually refuses to accept leadership responsibilities. Effective team leaders empower members and wait for members to help. They proactively work to build trust on the team. They don't unilaterally make decisions. They build group pride through a solid foundation of measurable productivity.

Methods, Processes and Procedures. The team has defined and adopted procedures for decision-making, problem-solving, process improvement, meetings and normal work activities. The team is effectively using and improving these procedures. A stellar team I worked with excelled by putting methods, processes and procedures in place early in the team's life, routinely reviewed them and amended them as the need arose. They included a large amount of training up front for ground rules, problem-solving methodologies and other processes and procedures so people had some clear definition about how to go about doing work on the team.

Interaction and Communication. Team members utilize appropriate and effective techniques and skills for interacting, influencing, giving and receiving feedback, facilitating team activities and resolving conflicts.

I have worked in team environments in which interaction and communication are very open. The high-performance teams I have seen give plenty of positive feedback to each other and look toward the common goals of the group. They will freely confront their conflicts if things aren't going well by providing feedback in a constructive manner. In this effective environment, team members receive feedback in an open manner. They don't get defensive and they actively listen to other members or to their leader before responding.

The teams that have low member interaction are easy to spot. There is little communication or intentional feedback among members. When members meet, many of them may have their own hidden agendas. Conflicts may be suppressed or simply not dealt with. There can also be open hostility, with members attacking one another.

Talents and Capabilities. The team has the talents and skills to perform its current mission and is developing knowledge and skills on an ongoing basis. It is using team experts to develop other members. It values differences and uses the unique capabilities of each member. Members are developing multiskills to provide maximum flexibility.

Stellar teams often complete a team training needs assessment when they first form. This assessment outlines all of the skills and knowledge needed by members and identifies where a team's strengths and weaknesses lie. It becomes a developmental tool teams can use to ensure that members have the necessary background to perform the team tasks and accomplish goals. Superior self-managed teams learn to develop multitalented members through ongoing coaching and job rotation.

In companies I would characterize as less than stellar, people are thrown into the fire or asked to sink or swim as a team. They are provided little in the way of development. This can be particularly harmful to people whose only experience has been working on their own.

Climate or Team Environment. There is a warm and trusting climate or team environment that encourages and reinforces openness, active participation by all, creativity and risk-taking, reinforcement, respect, honesty, a willingness to surface and resolve conflicts, and commitment to the team. Obviously, creativity and risk-taking are prerequisites for teams such as reengineering teams who are commissioned to think "outside the box" and find radical and new solutions for major business processes.

When teams don't have such environments, creative solutions are likely to be few and far between. Team members are more likely to develop solutions that are more confined, acceptable, less risky, less conflict-laden and overall less productive and beneficial to the organization. Commitment to these kinds of solutions is usually minimal.

Intergroup Relations. The team has formed cooperative working relationships with other teams, customers and suppliers, support groups, resource providers, and the organization's experts to meet the broader needs of external customers and the organization. The members have taken teaming to a new, higher level that enables them to stay focused on the external environment and identify resources, to continue learning and to continuously improve. One financial business I worked with made sharing among regional self-directed teams a priority. Even the company theme (SHARED SKILLS, SHARED SUCCESS) supported the effort.

Summing Up

Teams go through progressive stages of development until they reach a level of high performance and effectiveness. In the early stages, teams are dependent on the leader for direction, development and facilitation. In the later stages of development, the team relies on the leader for advice and coaching while team members provide leadership. Development is not a straight line. Teams will reach plateaus and occasionally regress as a result of changes in team membership and internal or environmental stresses on the team.

Understanding the stages of development and being able to recognize your team's current stage helps you as a team member or team leader to promote and enhance development to higher stages of performance. Effective stellar teams are defined by a number of criteria for success. Use these criteria to assess your team's effectiveness and performance.

Workbook Section

Practice

Team Leader

After you and the team members complete the Team Effectiveness and Performance Assessment (see instructions under Team Members), facilitate a discussion of each member's perception based on the assessment ratings.

Attempt to reach consensus agreement of the rating on each item. Discuss and reach agreement on items on which individual assessments differed by more than one point.

Differences of one point are not considered significant at this time. If differences are one or less, simply average them.

For those criteria assessed as three or less, develop and reach agreement on an improvement plan. If resource needs exist for improvement actions, inform the team how you might assist them.

Using the last part of the assessment, discuss the team's assessment of their current stage of development based on the consensus ratings. Reconcile the differences and modify your development plan as needed.

With the team, develop a methodology for monitoring performance compare with the plan.

Team Members

Complete the following Team Effectiveness and Performance Assessment.

Directions: For each statement, use the five-point scale described below and circle the number that most closely corresponds to your personal perception of your team. After completing the questionnaire, summarize the results on the last page.

1 = Not at all true for my team
2 = A little true for my team
3 = Somewhat true for my team
4 = Mostly true for my team
5 = Very true for my team

PURPOSE

- Our team has defined its mission, direction and goals. 1 2 3 4 5
- Our team members understand our team's mission, direction and goals. 1 2 3 4 5
- Our team is working towards accomplishing its mission and goals. 1 2 3 4 5
- Our team accepts and is committed to its mission, direction and goals. 1 2 3 4 5
- The mission, direction and goals of our team are aligned with those of the organization. 1 2 3 4 5
- Our team has defined and clearly understands its domain. 1 2 3 4 5

ROLES AND RESPONSIBILITIES

- Our team periodically redefines each member's roles and responsibilities. 1 2 3 4 5
- We clearly understand our individual roles and responsibilities. 1 2 3 4 5
- To avoid limiting each team member's roles and responsibilities, we rotate tasks periodically to keep up our skills. 1 2 3 4 5
- Our team looks for ways to expand roles and responsibilities for each individual and for the team as a whole. 1 2 3 4 5

LEADERSHIP

- Our team leader provides sufficient, appropriate, and effective leadership that meets our team's needs at this time. 1 2 3 4 5
- Our team leader encourages leadership from the team on a shared basis and serves more as a coach. 1 2 3 4 5
- Each member of the team is capable and provides leadership when it is needed. 1 2 3 4 5
- Leadership has emerged from within the team. We are becoming less dependent on our team

leader. 1 2 3 4 5

METHODS, PROCESSES, PROCEDURES

- Our team defined who will be involved in decision-making and the decision-making style for the different types of decisions our team makes. 1 2 3 4 5
- Our team uses a rational decision-making process for the decisions we make. 1 2 3 4 5
- We are working on improving our decision-making skills. 1 2 3 4 5
- Our team has defined and analyzed our improvement processes. 1 2 3 4 5
- Our team uses the systematic problem-solving or improvement process and techniques when necessary. 1 2 3 4 5
- Our team is reasonably skilled at and comfortable with the systematic problem-solving or process improvement process and techniques. 1 2 3 4 5
- We are working on improving our skills and comfort level with the problem-solving or improvement process and techniques. 1 2 3 4 5
- Our team meets regularly, and whenever necessary, to discuss our work, share information, plan, solve problems, etc. 1 2 3 4 5
- Our team meetings are planned and organized—we stick to the agenda and accomplish our business without wasting time. 1 2 3 4 5
- Everyone on our team prepares for and participates in team meetings, and everyone follows up on assignments. 1 2 3 4 5
- Our team has defined procedures that members follow to accomplish our team's work. 1 2 3 4 5
- Our team has set ways to evaluate our performance and control our processes and outputs. 1 2 3 4 5

INTERACTION AND COMMUNICATION

- Most team members demonstrate effective interaction skills and practices. 1 2 3 4 5

- Most team members practice good listening skills and try not to talk all the time. 1 2 3 4 5
- It is a common practice to give corrective and positive feedback to other team members. 1 2 3 4 5
- Feedback from team members is typically helpful, specific and given effectively. 1 2 3 4 5
- When conflicts arise, we try to deal with them effectively and appropriately. 1 2 3 4 5
- When conflicts come up, we follow a process to diagnose, discuss and resolve the issues. 1 2 3 4 5
- Our team members are skilled at influencing each other and others with whom we need to work. 1 2 3 4 5
- Our team is capable of facilitating our own discussions and activities. 1 2 3 4 5
- If it appears that our team is not making progress or is approaching something the wrong way, someone on the team will bring it to everyone's attention and suggest or encourage an alternative. 1 2 3 4 5

TALENTS AND CAPABILITIES

- We have a good mix of skills and talents on this team. 1 2 3 4 5
- Our members have the necessary technical skills and knowledge to perform their work and handle a variety of assignments effectively. 1 2 3 4 5
- Our team continually works at developing the skills and capabilities of all members. 1 2 3 4 5
- We have developed the administrative and interpersonal skills to manage our processes and work together as a team. 1 2 3 4 5
- We recognize and value the unique capabilities and approaches of all team members and try to capitalize on those differences. 1 2 3 4 5

CLIMATE OR TEAM ENVIRONMENT

- There is a high level of trust on our team. 1 2 3 4 5
- There is a high level of openness and honesty on our team. 1 2 3 4 5
- We encourage creativity and reasonable risk-taking on our team. 1 2 3 4 5
- Team members provide encouragement, support and reinforcement to one another. 1 2 3 4 5
- Team members treat each other with a high level of respect. 1 2 3 4 5
- All members are committed to the team. 1 2 3 4 5
- Conflicts are recognized and resolved in a positive, productive way. 1 2 3 4 5
- Everyone is encouraged and feels free to participate in team activities. 1 2 3 4 5

INTERGROUP RELATIONS

- Our team has a good relationship with other teams and others in the organization we depend upon for advice, assistance, resources, support or process inputs. 1 2 3 4 5
- Our team works with other teams and members of this organization to address problems and improvements that cut across the organization. 1 2 3 4 5
- Our team meets with our customers and suppliers periodically to stay on top of requirements, receive and give feedback, and look for ways to improve our products and services. 1 2 3 4 5
- We are clear on our team's domain and constantly review it in conjunction with other teams to reduce variances. 1 2 3 4 5
- Our team looks for opportunities to take on additional tasks or responsibilities that would add value to our products or services without threatening the other teams or individuals who may currently be responsible for those tasks or responsibilities. 1 2 3 4 5

Directions for the Comparison

Record the total score for each section (Purpose, Roles and Responsibilities, etc.). Then divide by the number of items in each section to obtain an average for each section.

Review where the strengths and improvement opportunities lie based on the section averages. (Look for peaks and valleys based on all members' averages for categories.)

Key Tips

Do your best to provide and seek clarity in the early stages of your team's life. It may help you become more effective more quickly.

Don't get upset if some conflict develops on your team; it may simply be part of your team's development and evolution.

Make sure you do an early inventory of your team's developmental needs.

Make an effort to promote trust and communication on your team. Positively reinforce members when they're doing things right.

It's a good idea to periodically assess your team's progress against stellar standards. Ongoing evaluation can help move you along the road to high performance. It will also help to create an environment that team members enjoy and one that makes your team a key contributor to your company's success.

12

THE GRAND FINALE

Unless you are a member of a natural work team or ongoing self-directed team, you're likely to face a time when the improvement initiative or project comes to an end. This happens when the improvement has been implemented and firmly entrenched in the company or simply when the project is completed. In either of these situations, your team has reached its ending point and will dissolve.

Often the end of a team is a time of mixed emotions for its members. They are looking forward to transitioning back to their normal jobs or some redesigned job as a result of a reengineering initiative. However, in many cases, team members have bonded and developed some intimate friends during the extensive—and intensive—time they spent together on the project.

As you approach this final stage, there are some things you should do to ensure that your team's efforts don't fall to pieces. Some of these considerations may differ depending on whether your team is a project, continuous improvement or reengineering team. It is important to take action before the team begins its victory celebration (something we'll discuss later) and officially disbands.

Project Team

If you have carefully progressed through the various stages of project management such as defining, planning, scheduling and monitoring, your project has reached its goals and your improvement initiatives have been successfully launched. In many cases, if you have not yet done so, you need to identify people to take over any ongoing processes necessary to maintain the project's output.

For example, before a drug manufacturer disbands its project team after a successful launch of a new product, the team members must identify and act upon any transitional issues to enable the employees who will assume the ongoing management of that drug to do so in a smooth and efficient manner. This might include educating employees about the project team's action during the project, reviewing the team's findings with employees as a result of the pilot project and sharing other information that will help the company continue to succeed with the new venture. The team must also relay data that could help identify potential problems or risks that might affect the success of project outcomes in the future.

Continuous Improvement

Most of the companies in which I have facilitated continuous improvement teams have built the necessary transitional steps into the final stages of their step-by-step continuous improvement systems. However, providing the organization with incremental improvements is of equally critical importance to an improvement team's successful conclusion. After all, you have spent a significant amount of time analyzing customer needs, analyzing workflows and successfully implementing solutions to improve processes. You don't want to see that work go to waste and see people reverting to old work habits with old workflow problems reappearing. You want to hold the gains the team has made.

Another issue continuous improvement teams need to be aware of is that customer requirements change. To ensure that improvements continue to meet the needs of the customer, they must be monitored by someone after the continuous improvement team disbands. One pharmaceutical organization uses a six-step methodology. In the sixth and final step, team members are asked to develop a plan that includes monitoring in order to ensure the continuation of improvement after the team dissolves.

At this phase, it is important to identify a process owner, the person who will be assigned responsibility for ongoing management of the new and improved process. Many times, this person has been the leader or a member of the continuous improvement team. It is crucial that the processes and process owners are clearly identified on the company Intranet so that there is no confusion about who is responsible.

Reengineering

As reengineering teams begin to wrap things up, they have a number of alternative issues to consider. One of my clients in the financial services area had a team spend a few business quarters just redesigning workflows and developing solutions for reengineered critical core business processes.

By establishing implementation teams, members of the reengineering team were able to ensure that key components of their reengineering effort, such as training, information systems and reward systems, were successfully put into effect. The separate implementation teams made sure that the reengineering team's plan had the specific personnel and resources necessary for success assigned to it.

Reengineering teams usually design and initiate massive changes within their organizations. Because much of the progress resulting from these radical changes may not be realized for some time, reengineering teams must build into their transition plans follow-up monitoring systems to keep track of the forward movement of their initiatives.

Reengineering teams at a major telecommunications firm designed new workflows with self-directed teams responsible for day-to-day workflows. Before it disbanded, the team developed a plan for a renewal team to be formed one year later to evaluate the progress of its original design and implementation efforts, and continuously improve upon those efforts.

Documented Record–A Piece of History

At its conclusion, the team should make sure it has documented evidence of its work. Information concerning its data gathering efforts, analysis, conclusions, solutions and implementation efforts can be helpful in case the company needs to explore other pursuits. This information can also be a valuable learning tool for other teams.

It never fails to surprise me to learn that, in some companies, teams merely file their information or discard their records. The most successful companies share their teams' efforts and have the information available for others to review.

One multinational pharmaceutical client sponsors quality award contests that reinforce good record keeping by continuous improvement team efforts. The company also shares winning efforts with the entire company worldwide. This company and others with which I have worked use documented storyboard forms to serve as trackable step-by-step records of their teams' efforts and process improvement methodologies (see Figure 12-1).

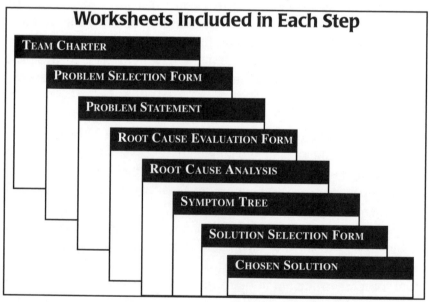

Worksheets Included in Each Step

TEAM CHARTER

PROBLEM SELECTION FORM

PROBLEM STATEMENT

ROOT CAUSE EVALUATION FORM

ROOT CAUSE ANALYSIS

SYMPTOM TREE

SOLUTION SELECTION FORM

CHOSEN SOLUTION

Figure 12-1. Storyboard forms

These storyboards provide great visual summaries of team efforts over several months.

Many software programs used by teams for project management may also be tools for logging the history of a team. These programs make the information easy to store and access by others as needed.

Reengineering teams usually keep information in large binders containing information such as customer requirements analysis, workflow findings and employee satisfaction surveys as well as recommendations and implementation plans. These binders are the archives of the team; they should be preserved and made available to others. At one company, a year after the reengineering team's solutions were used and its targets were set, renewal teams used its fact-filled binders as background material to review and track the progress of these solutions and the company's movement toward the targets.

Teams that have done a good job at communicating with the company from the design and analysis phases through implementation have usually found creative ways of documenting and conveying information. They use in-house newsletters, videotapes and other media.

The Final Evaluation

Although not every team experience has been good, I have participated in teams whose work was positive, productive, energizing and satisfying. Regardless of the outcome, it is important for every team to assess itself at its conclusion. In its final meetings, the team should review:

Its progress in attaining the initiative's goals

The process used in doing the work

What the team learned from its experiences working together

Next steps

Personal experiences and insights from working together.

A summary discussion will provide some of the closure needed after close teamwork. It can also serve a great learning experience. Team members often gain some valuable personal insights that they can use to improve their own performance levels in the future.

Celebration

When the team is dissolving it is important to acknowledge and celebrate each member's contributions. One company's research and development unit follows a five-step project management methodology to ensure that all vital areas are covered before its teams dissolve. The last step is designated Reward and Celebrate.

At a final celebration session, each person's contribution and the team's success is recognized. This acknowledgment is in the form of verbal or written testimonies for each team member and its leader based on reflections of all. Testimonies may also be solicited from internal or external customers.

Teams shouldn't wait until they are ready to disband before they celebrate. They should make time to acknowledge and enjoy the interim successes they achieve as they progress toward their major goals.

Typical celebrations are cookouts, sporting events, visits to restaurants, a series of team games or presentations of certificates from key leaders in the organization.

On one reengineering team I facilitated, it was decided to have a meeting at a hotel on the beach in Carmel, California. It had been several months since the team had begun its design and it was well on target as far as schedule and contributions. As a way to provide some R&R for team members, a celebration was held on the beach. During the celebration, the group loosened up and had fun with three-legged races, individual contests involving sweeping balls with brooms along the sand and across the finish line, and races requiring team members to hold an egg on a spoon. The relaxed and genial atmosphere contributed greatly to the team's success by providing relief from the tedious work. Also, it sparked additional camaraderie among team members. After the celebration, the team returned to their work refreshed, rejuvenated and with the renewed vigor that provided momentum to work through the final stages of its business process reengineering designs.

Debriefing Time

An important item on the agenda for a team during its final stage is to debrief members regarding their experiences working together. An easy method for debriefing is the evaluation method described in Chapter 4 that uses a piece of easel paper divided into two columns. One column is marked with a + (plus) sign, the other with a delta (Δ). Feedback is solicited from the members about accomplishments of which they are particularly proud and key contributions and their perception of the team's key contributions. Note these comments on the + side. Then ask the members what mistakes they believe the team made and what could be done differently in the future. Note these comments on the Δ (change) side.

Often some storyboarding technique or ideas using parts of an affinity diagram tool will be used. Team members write ideas on Post-it notes or index cards or respond to questions like "How did we do?" Notes are posted and organized under themes. I like to use a silent technique where members, without talking to one another, continue to move noted ideas around on a chart or wall until the entire group agrees with the organized rows that several ideas are grouped under. Then the group discusses category headings to ensure agreement on the basic categories. Team members read their notes, responding to clarifying questions as they discuss their perceptions. Often the main ideas or themes are summarized.

Another less formal approach is simply to ask each member of the team to give their verbal reflections of how the team performed.

Special Closing Ceremonies

In many cases, a team's closing will mark a transition for the organization in terms of how it does business. Whether the transition encompasses a redesigned process or a movement to self-direction, it is often symbolized in team closing ceremonies. For example, in one reengineering team ceremony, each team member took a symbol (e.g., a hierarchical organization chart) from the old organization and threw it in a trash can. By the end of the ceremony, the can was filled with various symbols to denote that the company was discarding various components of its old image and replacing them with newly designed improvements.

Revisiting Millennium Models— Final Words and Cautions

Millennium Model 1: Emphasis on Quality and Service

When considering the elements of the Millennium Model (chapter 1), it is imperative for the team to make certain that transition plans are in place for ownership, responsibility and corrective action, if necessary, for the project or improvement it has launched. The team should establish monitoring measures and methods to enable the party designated to implement the new initiatives or improvements.

Millennium Model 2: More with Less

In order for the team to maximize its worth to the company, it should identify where additional opportunities lie or other improvement opportunities may exist. This could lead to the establishment of additional problem-solving teams or improvement teams that look at high-payback areas that may not have been within the initial charter. If the organization plans to remain competitive and accomplish more with less, workflows that cause the company problems and waste costly resources must be improved.

While investigating and analyzing their own chartered workflows, teams often identify areas requiring improvement outside their immediate boundaries. It is important that teams communicate these potential opportunities to key leaders in their companies in any final documentation and during official closings. By identifying waste, teams can help their companies maintain a continuous improvement culture.

Millennium Model 3: People Development and Utilization

Many actions proposed by teams have an impact on how jobs throughout the organization are developed and how people interact. Therefore, it is important that the team complete a change management plan isolating and identifying potential areas of support as well as likely areas of resistance. In any transition, key actions should be developed to help ensure that resistance factors are adequately addressed. Obviously the best way to counter resistance to change is to make sure that people are given the training and development for whatever change in behavior and skills will be required to use the new solutions.

People-oriented organizations may even develop a whole new set of key competencies that will be needed for any new positions that may be needed in the new structures or workflows. These organizations also create training and development plans to help people make major work transitions. Any team's best and most well-planned efforts can be wasted if people aren't provided with the training to give them the new knowledge and experience needed and to make them comfortable with their changing roles and responsibilities. Outgoing teams may conduct assessments as part of their transition plans to determine people's comfort and capabilities about new structures and functions, processes or job requirements.

Millennium Model 4: Process Control and Structure

Before they dissolve, the best teams see to it that proper communications plans are in place to ensure that everyone within the organization is aware of the new workflows and that the proper structures are in place for monitoring and maintaining control. Communication plans may include technology used to ensure that everyone is aware of the new standard operating procedures. Charts and other visual data displays may be posted to help the new teams keep track of progress or identify problems.

Millennium Model 5: Team-Based Work Systems

Let's say, in its quest for radical change, a major process reengineering team stumbles on some problems with some backroom processes that support major business workflows. If the team has the best interests of the company in mind, it should identify opportunities for incremental improvement presented by these problems to the key people within the organization who can do something about them.

It is also important that when a reengineering team submits a proposal to move into self-directed structures, it needs to be sure that long-term plans are in place to educate employees and facilitate the transition. This is particularly true in organizations in which people have spent the last 15 or 20 years taking direction from others.

Requirements for a Successful Shift to Management

In a recent issue of *Inc. Magazine,* writer John Case makes a convincing argument for what an organization needs to do to encourage employees learn to think like owners. According to Case, an organization must:

Structure the company so that people at all levels are encouraged to make decisions. People at all levels need decision-making authority.

Share key financial information with all employees regularly and frequently. People must have the information they need to make intelligent decisions. Many companies now are using a balanced scorecard to help them gather financial as well as other information on the performance of the organization. A standardized set of measures is shared with the entire organization on an ongoing basis.

Train people to understand the financial information that governs the business. Teams gain some of this knowledge when they assign costs for activity steps in their workflows.

Give people a stake in the results of their decisions and in the company itself. The structure of the self-directed team itself will help, but for the company to succeed with this self-directed concept it must have five key elements. These are:

Element 1: Organizational leadership focused on empowerment. Self-managed teams need well-thought-out, clearly communicated and closely followed visions, missions, guiding principles, strategies and priorities that encourage and support empowerment, ownership, customer focus, process management, teamwork and people development.

Element 2: Management style that supports, not suffocates. Self-managed teams need a style of management that delegates authority and responsibility, and embraces empowerment and semi-autonomy. Management must support, reinforce and offer help when it's needed.

Element 3: A dedicated empowerment process. Self-managed teams need an organization dedicated to empowerment that provides well-defined roles and responsibilities, unambiguous standards and boundaries, skill and knowledge development, time for team-building, access to resources, direct feedback systems, supportive policies and a reward system that compensates employees for their skills, knowledge, performance and contribution.

Element 4: Capable committed teams. Self-managed teams require shared leadership, effective teamwork, a range of talents and skills, and commitment to team development, performance, and work, as well as commitment to the philosophy and methodology of improvement.

Element 5: Dedication to a continuous improvement process. Self-managed teams must be dedicated to continuous improvement. They must always look for ways to make processes function more efficiently, with fewer errors and so on. Teams must routinely evaluate their performance to determine where improvement is necessary, plan for the improvement, commit the time and resources to improvement, take action steps to improve and then monitor the results of their actions.

Summing Up

No matter what type of team you are on, there are some considerations to think about as you close up the shop. Carefully assess how you might keep your team's information for future reference, how you might share that information, and what plans you need to put in place so that your efforts aren't wasted and the gains you made as a team are sustained.

Don't forget to take some time for evaluating the entire team initiative. It can be a great learning experience.

Keep the Millennium Models in mind as you transition back to your old or new assignments. It will help keep you focused on sustained improvement.

If you are considering some new self-directed structures, make sure that the organizational systems are there to support these new teams in your company.

> *Reengineer is a word that engenders fear.*
> *Downsize will terrorize those who don't realize*
> *What was, isn't; what is, won't be.*
> *And constant change is the only reality*
> *And business is in a constant upheaval*
> *And although very trying, it is not evil.*
> *So welcome change, make it your friend*
> *For in every change there's a hidden dividend.*
>
> —Sid Madwed[1]

Workbook Section

Practice

TEAM LEADER

At a closing meeting, facilitate a discussion with the team to evaluate itself. Write the following items on separate flip charts:

"I am most pleased that this team...."

"I wish that this team had...."

"My key discovery from this team experience was...."

Have the team members respond to these questions either by reviewing each item individually or by soliciting a response for each item spontaneously by each member.

Lead a discussion of what the team could do differently in a different team situation. Summarize the key themes on a flip chart.

Review the final words and cautions associated with each Millennium Model. Use this information as a final checklist for the team. Ask the team whether all the necessary transition work has been put in place including: transition plans for ownership, communication of additional opportunities, organization commitment and development plans, communication plans for new workflows, company support for new team-based systems. Note any additional items on an action list that develops from this discussion and implement them.

TEAM MEMBERS

Each team member should write his or her name on the top of an easel paper and post the paper on the wall. Using a separate Post-it note or index card for each individual, write a statement that you feel provides some recognition to each team member. After each member has completed his or her statements, place the card or Post-it note under the appropriate chart for each team member. Maybe you even want to write one for yourself.

After reviewing all of the statements that were posted under your name, go around the team and have each member share his or her reflections of the statements. Don't forget to share your own thoughts.

Key Points

Don't just end the team. Take time to get closure on your assignments. Take some time to reflect on the experience.

Take time to celebrate. After all, if you have reached an ending experience, you have probably put some considerable time and effort into your project, problem or improvement initiative. Be creative about how you might celebrate. Maybe do something most of the team members have never done before—perhaps something like rock climbing or bungee jumping!

Make sure you have done the planning necessary for a successful transition. Sustaining something is often harder than getting it off the ground in the first place.

Make sure you keep a record of your work. Some of the most successful teams condense their thick binders of information into a succinct *"Reader's Digest* version."

Based on feedback from your team members and leader, make an action plan of what you might do the next time a team opportunity presents itself. What could you do differently or better? You might as well use this experience to your advantage.

Some Final Thoughts

As we move into the next millennium, remember that teams are not a passing fad. They're here to stay! Right this minute, progressive companies are already trying to get more with less and are focusing on many of those Millennium Models in an effort to stay competitive. We also have some powerful evidence of the positive impact of teams, whether they are continuous improvement, virtual, cross-functional, project or problem-solving. Many companies have already witnessed some excellent results that have had a significant impact on their employees, customers and, of course, the bottom line.

Even if you have already embarked on teaming in your company, this book can serve as reinforcement of what you have done right and as a checklist for future endeavors and as a comprehensive framework for starting, continuing and ending teams. It is a resource and a guide to insights from the field, from other team experiences and from my own observations. The workbook exercises provide valuable practice—use them as you see fit depending on the type of team you are working with and its maturity.

Although individual teams may live out their lives and finally dissolve, teaming for improvement is a never-ending process. Take the bits and pieces you need to make your next team experience a fun and productive enterprise.

As that famous cowboy hero Roy Rogers might have said to all you teammates out there, "Happy Trails to You."

NOTES

Chapter 1

1. Ken Blanchard and Sheldon Bowles, *Gung Ho!* (New York: William Morrow and Company, 1998.) Copyright 1998 by Blanchard Family Partnership and Ode to Joy, Ltd.
2. Bill Brewer, ed., "The Virtual World of R&D," *News for a Change* (Cincinnati, Ohio: AQP, May 1998), 7. Permission to reprint granted by AQP. Copyright 1998. All rights reserved.
3. Kara Choquette, "Streamlined Surgery Is Win-Win Situation," *USA Today*, 1 May 1998, section B, 5. Copyright 1998, USA Today. Reprinted with permission.
4. Susan Cohen and Gerald E. Ledford, Jr., "The Effectiveness of Self-Managing Teams: A Quasi-Experiment," *Human Relations*, Vol. 47 (New York: Plenum Publishing Corp., 1994).
5. For more on Sam Walton's views on teams, see: Sam Walton with John Huey, *Sam Walton Made in America, My Story* (New York: Doubleday/Random House, 1993).
6. Del Jones, "GE Turns Decision Making Art into Science," *USA Today*, 1 May 1998, section B, 5.
7. "Subarctic Survival Situation" is copyrighted by Human Synergistics, Inc. Copies are available from the publisher at 39819 Plymouth Road C8020, Plymouth, Michigan 48170-8020. The publisher can be reached by telephone at (734) 459-1030 or by facsimile at (734) 459-5557.

Chapter 2

1. Stephen R. Covey, *The Seven Habits of Highly Effective People* (New York, Simon & Schuster, 1989). "Begin With The End in Mind"™ is a trademark of Franklin Covey Co. Used with permission. All rights reserved.
2. *1997 AQP Conference Highlights and Team Winners Presentations* (Cincinnati, AQP, 1997).
3. *1996 AQP Conference Highlights and Team Winners Presentations* (Cincinnati, AQP, 1996).

Chapter 3
1. Ibid.

Chapter 7
1. Ibid.
2. The Buzan Organization has kindly granted permission to use Mind Maps in this publication. The Buzan Centers may be contacted at 1-800-YMINDMA; by e-mail at BUZAN000@aol.com; or at www.Mind-Map.com.

Chapter 9
1. Barbara Pate Glacel, "Teamwork's Top Ten Lead to Quality," *Journal on Quality and Participation,* Vol. 20, No. 1 (January/February 1997). Reprinted with permission from the Association for Quality and Participation, Cincinnati, Ohio. All rights reserved. For more information call AQP at (513) 381-1959.

Chapter 10
1. For an updated review of Maslow see Ron Zemke, review of "Maslow for a New Millennium," in *Training Magazine* (December 1998), 55-58.
2. For more information on McClelland's three social motives of achievement and power, see Motives, Personality and Society, *Selected Papers* (Praeger, 1984).

Chapter 12
1. Copyright and used by permission of the author, Sidney Madwed, a fellow member of National Speakers Association. He may be contacted at Sid@madwed.com or http://www.madwed.com or (203) 372-6484.

BIBLIOGRAPHY

Blanchard, Ken, and Sheldon Bowles. *Gung Ho!* New York: William Morrow and Company, Inc., 1998.

Block, Peter. *The Empowered Manager: Positive Political Skills at Work.* San Francisco: Jossey-Bass, 1987.

Berry, Thomas H. *Managing the Total Quality Transformation.* New York: McGraw-Hill, 1991.

Brewer, Bill, ed. "The Virtual World of R&D." *News for a Change.* Association for Quality and Participation, July 1998, p. 7.

Carnevale, Anthony P., Leila J. Gainer, and Eric Schultz. *Training the Technical Work Force.* San Francisco: Jossey-Bass, 1990.

Choquette, Kara K. "Team Approach Wins Points with Workers." *USA Today,* May 1, 1998, p. 5B.

— —. "Streamlined Surgery is Win-Win Situation." *USA Today,* May 1, 1998, p. 5B.

Covey, Stephen R. *The Seven Habits of Highly Effective People.* New York: Simon & Schuster, 1989.

Cragan, John F., and David W. Wright. *Communication In Small Group Discussions.* Third ed., St. Paul, Minn.: West, 1991.

Dalziel, Murray M., and Stephen C. Schoonover. *Changing Ways: A Practical Tool for Implementing Change within an Organization.* New York: Amacom, 1988.

Deming, W. Edwards. *Out of the Crisis.* Cambridge, Mass.: MIT Press, 1986.

Douglass, Merrill E., and Donna N. Douglass. *Time Management for Teams.* New York: Amacom, 1992.

Eldridge, Earle. "Enterprising Team Solves TVA Coal Problems." *USA Today,* May 1, 1998, p. 4B.

Fisher, K. Kim. "Management Roles in the Implementation of Participative Management Systems." *Human Resource Management* 25 (Fall 1986): 456–79.

Frances, Dave, and Don Young. *Improving Work Groups—A Practical Manual for Team Building.* San Diego: University Associates, 1979.

Galagan, Patricia. "Work Teams That Work." *Training and Development Journal,* November 1986, pp. 33-35.

Garvin, David. "Quality Problems, Policies and Attitudes in the U.S. and Japan: An Exploratory Study." *Academy of Management Journal* 29 (December 1986): 653–73.

Glacel, Barbara Pate. "Teamwork's Top Ten Lead to Quality." *Journal on Quality and Participation,* 20.1 (January/February 1997).

Hackman, J. Richard, ed. *Groups That Work and "Those Who Don't": Creating Conditions for Effective Teamwork.* San Francisco: Jossey-Bass, 1990.

Hanna, David. *Designing Organizations for High Performance.* Reading, Mass.: Addison-Wesley, 1989.

Hoerr, John. "The Payoff from Teamwork." *Business Week,* July 10, 1989, pp. 56-62.

Hughes, Frieda, with Ned Hamson. "AQP's 1997 Excellence Awards." *Journal on Quality and Participation,* 20.4 (September 1997): 36-40.

Jablonski, Joseph R. *Implementing Total Quality Management— Competing in the 1990's.* Albuquerque: Technical Management Consortium, 1990.

Jones, Del. "GE Turns Decision-Making 'Art Into Science'." *USA Today,* May 1, 1998, p. 5B.

Kanter, Rosabeth Moss. *Change Masters.* New York: Simon and Schuster, 1983.

— —. *When Giants Learn to Dance.* New York: Simon and Schuster, 1989.

Kilmann, Ralph H. Managing *Beyond the Quick Fix—A Completely Integrated Program for Creating and Maintaining Organizational Success.* San Francisco: Jossey-Bass, 1989.

Lawler, Edward E. III. *High Involvement Management.* San Francisco: Jossey-Bass, 1986.

Litwin, George and Robert A. Stringer, Jr. *Motivation and Organizational Climate.* 6th ed., Cambridge, Mass.: Harvard University Press, 1981.

Napier, Rodney W., and Matti K. Gershenfeld. *Groups: Theory and Practice.* Fourth ed. Boston: Houghton Mifflin, 1989.

Orsburn, Jack D., Linda Moran, Ed Musselwhite, and John H. Zenger. *Self-Directed Work Teams*. Homewood, Ill.: Business One Irwin, 1990.

Pasmore, William A., and John J. Sherwood. *Sociotechnical Systems*. San Diego: University Associates, 1978.

Peters, Tom. *Thriving On Chaos*. New York: Harper and Row, 1987.

Rees, Fran. *How to Lead Work Teams*. San Diego: Pfeiffer and Co., 1991.

Rosen, Ned. *Teamwork and the Bottom Line*. Hillsdale, N.J.: Lawrence Erlbaum Associates, 1989.

Rubenstein, Sidney P. "Don't Fear the Team—Join It." *New York Times,* June 11, 1989, sec.3, p. 2.

Simmons, John, and Geri Blitzman. "Training for Self-Managing Work Teams." *Quality Circles Journal,* 9 (December 1986): 18-21.

Snow, Harrison. *The Power of Team Building*. San Diego: Pfeiffer and Co., 1992.

Scherkenbach, William W. *The Deming Route to Quality and Productivity—Road Maps and Roadblocks*. Privately printed, n.d.

Schonberger, Richard J. *Japanese Manufacturing Techniques*. New York: Free Press, 1982.

Townsend, Patrick L., and Joan E. Gebhardt. *Commit to Quality*. New York: John Wiley and Sons, 1986.

Tunks, Roger. *Fast Track to Quality—A 12-Month Program for Small- to Mid-Sized Businesses*. New York: McGraw-Hill, 1992.

Varney, Glenn H. *Building Productive Teams*. San Francisco: Jossey-Bass, 1989.

Walton, Sam and John Huey. *Sam Walton Made in America, My Story*. New York: Bantam Books, 1993.

Weisbord, Marvin R. *Productive Workplaces: Organizing and Managing for Dignity, Meaning and Community*. San Francisco: Jossey-Bass, 1987.

Woodyard, Chris. "University Takes Pain out of Parking Passes." *USA Today,* May 1, 1998, p. 4B.

Zemke, Ron. Review of "Maslow for a New Millennium."
Training Magazine, December 1998, pp. 55-58.
"1997 AQP Conference Highlights–Gold, Silver and Bronze
Winners and Presentations," produced by the Association
for Quality and Participation, 1997.
"1996 AQP Conference Highlights and Team Winners
Presentations," produced by the Association for Quality
and Participation, 1996.

ABOUT THE AUTHOR

William G. Stieber, Ph.D. is President of InterPro Development, Inc., a training and organizational improvement consulting company. InterPro offers organizational design and development, and intervention—as well as training in leadership, team development, project and time management, process improvement and facilitation skills.

From an understanding of how organizations work, Dr. Stieber shows how you can use teams effectively to get results in the next millennium. He highlights important team leadership approaches that work, along with important tips for team members regardless of whether teams are used for incremental improvement, radical improvement or self-direction.

He has over twenty years of experience in financial service, health care, manufacturing and consulting fields. His recent accomplishments have involved two major redesigns of businesses, development and implementation of major team leader and team member initiatives, and design and implementation of leadership assessment and development processes in Fortune 500 companies. He has also facilitated organizational transitions to self-directed team environments. His clients include AT&T, Citibank, ICI Americas, Lockheed Martin, Merck and Co., SmithKline Beecham and Zeneca. Dr. Stieber has had adjunct assignments with New York University and the Philadelphia College of Textiles and Science.

His article "Building Teams for Change" was recently published in *Thriving on Change in Organizations*.

William Stieber may be contacted at:

800-933-6165
or
Bill.S@Stieber.com